Zero to Millionaire Real Estate Investor

A Millionaire Fastlane to Building Unlimited Wealth by Investing in Cheap Real Estate & Rental Property; Secrets to Becoming a Millionaire by Passive Income

Johnath S. Vines

© **Copyright 2020**

All Rights Reserved. No part of this book may be reproduced in any form without permission in writing from the author. Reviewers may quote brief passages in reviews.

Disclaimer: No part of this publication may be reproduced or transmitted in any form or by any means, mechanical or electronic, including photocopying or recording, or by any information storage and retrieval system, or transmitted by email without permission in writing from the publisher.

While all attempts have been made to verify the information provided in this publication, neither the author nor the publisher assumes any responsibility for errors, omissions, contrary interpretations of the subject matter herein, or liability whatsoever on behalf of the purchaser or reader of these materials.

Table of Contents

Table of Contents

Introduction

Chapter 1 – How You Can Access Free Assets when Getting Started
- Free Real Estate Investment Resources (Tools and Methods)
- Make Plans to Find Deals
- Discovering Potential Properties
  - Assessing Properties and Deciding Worth
  - Financing Your Properties
- Flipping and Renovation
- Property Rental and Management
- What Plans of Action are Available?

Chapter 2 – Finding Cheap Houses: Off-market Homes
- 5 Benefits of Buying Off-market Homes

Chapter 3 – Best Places to Buy Cheap Land, How Much Those Property Costs and Price Range
- Risk and Techniques When Thinking About Online Land Sales
- Cheap U.S Lands for Retirees to Invest In
- Differences between Building a House and Buying Land for Building a House

Chapter 4 – Investing in Real Estate with Little Money
- 15 Ways You Can Invest in Real Estate, Spending Little Money

Chapter 5 – Flipping: The Strategy for Continuous Real Estate Profits
- Upsides and Downsides of Flipping a House
- Step by Step Instructions to Begin House Flipping
- Common House-flipping Errors New Investors Make
- 7 Indications of a Bombed Flip

Chapter 6 – How to Use Online Resources; The Social Media Tool
- Real Estate Marketing Toolkit
- 10 Hints That Will Help You Improve Your Real Estate Advertising

Chapter 7 – Rental Properties: Where and How to Buy Your First Rental Property

Beginning Your Search
10 Important Features to Observe

Getting Information

Picking a Property

How to Determine Rent

Making the Purchase

Places You Can Purchase Rental Property

Chapter 8 – Strategic and Tactical Suggestions to Reduce the Cost of Managing Your Real Estate

Ways Investors and Property Managers are Controlling Costs
10 Ways to Manage Costs Forever

Chapter 9 – How to Buy Cheap Foreclosure

Ways for Investors to Discover Foreclosed Homes

Reason Foreclosed Homes are More Affordable

Is it Advisable to Purchase a Foreclosed Home?

Where to Discover Foreclosed Homes Today

Purchasing Foreclosed Homes: The Pros and Cons

Ways to Discover Foreclosed Homes

How to Purchase Foreclosures

Implication of Fewer Foreclosures on the Housing Market

Reasons It's Getting Harder to Discover Foreclosures

Find a Deal on Foreclosed Homes

Chapter 10 – Look at MLS Reports to Discover How Long a Property Has Been Listed

Ways to Determine the Cumulative DOM

Property Listings

Chapter 11 – Purchase Money: Mortgage/Seller Financing

Hard Money Loan versus Purchase Money Loan

Kinds of Purchase Money Loans

Definition of Purchase-Money Mortgage
How to Use the Purchase-Money Morgages

    In Purchase-Money Mortgage Agreements, What Happens to Existing Mortgages?
    The Dangers of Purchase-Money Mortgages

Ways to Qualify for a Loan with the Customary Lenders

Seller Financing
    The Mechanics of Seller Financing
    Kinds of Seller Financing Deals
    Getting Professional Help
    Tips to Minimize Seller Risk
    Negotiating the Loan
    Employing a Loan Service Company

Chapter 12 – How to Form Partnerships to Invest in Real Estate with Little Money

What is a RELP?
    Is the REIT Classified Among the Limited Partnership?
    The Commercial Partnerships in Real Estate
    Real Estate Partnership Taxation
    Pros and Cons of Real Estate Partnerships

Ways to Structure Your Real Estate Investment Partnership

Chapter 13 – How to Mitigate Financial Loss as Possible

Real Estate Investment Risks: Bad Returns

Real Estate Investment Risks: Depreciation

Real Estate Investment Risks Vacancies

Real Estate Investment Risks: Bad Tenants

Real Estate Investment Risks: Lack of Knowledge
    Search for Below-Market Rents when Purchasing
    Search for Advantageous Financing which Reduces Cash Outflow
    Increase Your Down Payment
    Search for Real Estate that You Can Profitably Improve
    Search for Future Hot Areas
    The Basic Ideology is to Purchase Value

Conclusion

Introduction

The real estate world is an alluring and progressive industry. This is an industry worth trillions of dollars today, and it will continue to increase in value simply because the land is an essential part of life. We all desire to have a roof over our heads, maybe our homes, our workplace, and so on. All these structures are developed with specific materials and for a particular reason. To be a successful real estate investor, you must understand the following concepts: economics, investment, and risk.

Theoretically, real estate investing is not as complicated as it is the same with planting. You invest money, allow it to grow, then after some time, you'll reap more money. However, you should know every investment requires a level of risk. Therefore the expected profit should cover the measure of risk involved. For example, consider a monopoly. To win, you first buy properties, evades bankruptcy, then gather the rent to buy more properties. That might seem oversimplified, but that's the case. However, any error in your investment strategy could prove fatal.

As an investor there are four things to always keep in mind; firstly, the real estate market can never end. Having a home is as essential as water, energy, food, and clothing in this age and time. Real estate investors are fundamental to keeping this crucial human need accessible and affordable. In nations where investing resources into real estate is restricted or controlled by the government like it was in former Communist Bloc nations, the masses suffer, and so those the land. Secondly, there are various ways for you to participate and succeed with real estate. For the vast majority, the only real estate investment they have is the place they live. Their house is their most significant investment. From 2000 to 2007, real estate boom, numerous newbies engaged with flipping houses—purchasing low then looking to sell high. As you probably are aware, innumerable flippers flopped and lost a lot. In investor terms, flipping is defined as hypothesizing and trading. People usually consider it as gambling. Although flipping is one investment strategy, there are more advanced, safer approaches to do well as a real estate investor. This book is loaded up with vital information that has helped many beginners succeed in their real estate journeys. As a person interested in making money from real estate, you're should be ready to invest instead of flipping, trading, speculating, or gambling. Thirdly, Real estate enables you to control your investments, but you need to learn the skills. In the unpredictable times of early 2009, many individuals were trillions of dollars; why? They gave over control of their riches to others. Indeed, even the incomparable Warren Buffett's asset, Berkshire Hathaway, lost 40% of its worth! (2008), Many lost their jobs, which implies they had no influence over their work either. Successful investors in this book have control over both their investment and business. They share both their sad and happy times with you. In this book, you'll discover how to control your investment as well as your financial destiny. The learning cycle is constant. Many so-called "monetary specialists" offer guidance in real estate who don't invest in land. In 1999, thanks to the "Dot-com" boom, the stock market was super hot. One particular investment specialist, a previous stockbroker, was shouting the praises of mutual funds and stocks. After the stock crash in 2001, the specialist unexpectedly reemerged with another book about real estate, declaring himself a real estate guru. His advice on real estate was not only appalling. As you might have guessed, when the real estate market crashed, he disappeared again. Many financial "specialists" know little of real estate, yet they talk seriously about it and declare it unsafe. The main reason why real estate would be dangerous to them is because of their lack of information. These folks usually suggest that people save and invest in mutual funds. For what reason do they recommend mutual funds and savings? The apparent reason is that most of these self-proclaimed specialists are sponsored by banks, the media, and mutual fund companies. This book will allow you to learn the nitty-gritty of real estate investment,

There are some practices you need to understand before you begin your real estate journey. REITs (Real Estate Investment Trusts) are probably the most effortless way to invest real estate without purchasing a physical property. These are managed by the SEC (Securities and Exchange Commission). REITs are a collective investment scheme as they pool assets from investors to obtain profitable real estate.

This arrangement is overseen by an expert who's responsible for ensuring maximum profit. Through REITs, an individual has an indirect share in real estate through "flow-through" (this means you own properties like there were direct investments)

REITs are bought through stockbrokers like when you're purchasing or selling shares. Another common practice is becoming a real estate agent. This is a decent option if you have little or no capital to kick off your real estate career. You can offer to help landowners find buyers. This is where you can begin to sharpen your marketing skills when you're ready to start life as a real estate investor fully. Being an agent implies you get a commission after you introduce buyers to the property. You can consider this an introduction to some things you need to learn because no information is wasted in a real estate investor's world. You can learn how to list the property to the public through banners, notification, fliers, etc. However, things have gotten simpler now with the advent of the internet and social media. Promoting properties on the web is the least demanding and least expensive technique to reach people. You can take purchasers to see the property and hone your negotiating skills.

Open space renting is one old practice whereby you seek to buy land in a decent location. This is key to your investment, and you must be very careful about it. After the purchase, you wait for the land's value to grow, then rent it out to mechanics, churches, and anyone who needs space to operate their business. The different organizations can develop a stopgap structure that can be effortlessly removed when you are prepared to sell.

Property development is a significant part of real estate investment that requires a big capital. It is about procuring devalued properties that can be renovated then leased or sold at a higher price. Just as is the case with all real estate investments, the importance of location cannot be overemphasized here. It is important to make sure the cost of developing will be far less than the selling price after the property has been renovated. For instance, if 2million was spent on renovation, you have to ensure you can sell the property for 4 million or thereabout. There are many things involved before you proceed to put resources into property development. All this will be discussed in the books.

Many real estate investors practice franchising, a splendid method to buy and hold land in various rapidly developing areas. It, however, requires extensive capital. This is as straightforward as when you obtain land and use it to set up a business, café, restaurant, and more. Afterward, you purchase land in different areas, construct your buildings then seek franchisees who can manage the eateries for you. You might think that brands like KFC, Mr. Biggs, McDonald's, Chicken Republic, and the likes are just into the food business. Be that as it may, Acquiring real estate is a significant piece of their business. These lands rapidly grow in value after some time. People are also buying/building rental properties, which is another substantial real estate investment; why? Because, if done right, you'll continue to earn until you die. All these standard practices demand that you know the right time and place to yield profit for you as an investor. As you must have realized by now, It's possible to invest in real estate without putting down any cash.

There are numerous ways for anyone to share the trillions of dollars in real estate; Seek to find the right information and tools. Therefore, you don't need to continue procrastinating till you've saved a significant amount of money before you can get a move on.

Real estate is one very stable investment that cannot get past you once you're following due process.

You have to get used to asking questions before you pay for any property. Likewise, ensure that you are dealing in and with a location that you're familiar with. When you're wiser and stronger as an investor, you can explore further. For instance, you don't want to purchase land in a region with a bad history, which suffers from flooding, or that doesn't have a decent road network. That could cause you many problems to get it sold. Also, it's not good to start your real estate investment journey on a bad record.

You also need to learn to distinguish areas. Some locations have a high potential to grow rapidly; others might have their value in the minerals resources they hold. Negotiating is another big part of real estate. To secure the best deals for yourself, you must learn the secrets of real estate negotiations. This is the one quality that separates a successful investor from the others. Even when you're told the cost of a property and the price falls within your budget, do not be in a rush to agree. One, you might be able to get the real estate for a lower cost, and two, there's nothing wrong about flexing your negotiating skills. A similar concept also applies when you are prepared to sell.

This book, Zero to millionaire real estate investor, is not just a book to share the concepts of real estate investments but a practical guide for the man or woman who's ready to act. There are many ideas involved in this venture, as is any venture that requires dealing with humans. However, in this book, we want to lay a solid groundwork for any individual who is tired of living from paycheck to paycheck.

Times are tough. These are times when even great economies are sinking into recession, and some even fall into depression. Working the standard 9-5 isn't helping anymore. Empowered with correct & consistent information, a practical plan, and the right mindset, you can break out of the "rat-race" as we know it. Just like any new journey that an individual embarks on, the beginning is always the most challenging hurdle. However, once you grasp how it all works, you'll be surprised at how easily you can play the game and how fun it is. Gone are the days of "cutting your coat according to your size," begging and getting immersed in debt. With real estate investment, you can:

- Build both your assets and your future

- Generate numerous streams of income for yourself, long after you've retired

- Take advantage of tax benefits

The possibilities are infinite because people will always need land; therefore, a real estate's value can only grow.

Chapter 1 – How You Can Access Free Assets when Getting Started

As a person interested in investing in real estate, you need to embrace technology's power and effectiveness. Technological innovations will make your real estate investment journey easier. Home leasing or buying is simpler and straightforward, limiting the chance of extortion or documental tricks. New companies, providing unique solutions, and help take care of existing issues, are constantly empowered to work on their specialty and succeed.

The real estate investment toolkits are utilized by private and business financial specialists to help study property to see whether it merits putting resources. Below is a rundown of tools you can use as a real estate investor when getting started.

Free Real Estate Investment Resources (Tools and Methods)

Here are the tools and strategies you can access to help ensure your property venture and capital. These also help you in making wiser investment decisions.

1. *Cash flow pro forma*: This tool is very important because the first things any smart investor looks at is the "cash flow projection." They check this before considering any potential property. The real estate pro forma enables you to assess the general productivity, considering the income, effective gross profit, operating expenses, possible gross profit, all expenses, and net operating and adjusted net operating income.

    For example, East Atlantic Inc. is kicking-off in it's first year with $90,000. To get the net change figure, you subtract estimated cash uses from the average cash sources. Let's say cash uses (operating cost, goods purchased) totals $25,000. Cash sources (from sales, etc) totals $29,000. Therefore net change (in cash position) is +$4000. After adding the start-up cash, East Atlantic begins it's next month with $94,000.

2. **DCF method (Discounted cash flow):** This technique involves valuing every money related resource, including real estate trade. It deals with the fundamental guideline that states that "cash has more worth right now than it will in the future." Also, the estimation of an asset is basically the value of all projected cash-flows that are limited to hazard. This strategy attempts to ascertain how viable a venture is by working out the extended future salary or income—afterward, discounting the cash-flow to arrive at an expected current estimation of the investment. For instance, let's assume there's an annual interest rate of 6% and $1 in a savings account, therefore the $1.05 DCF in a year.

The following variables should be incorporated in the real estate business: cost of interest rate, extra yearly costs, projected incomes, holding period, and the projected return on an investment after the property is sold. You should know that forecasting isn't a precise science, and DCF analysis is the best way to assess real estate risk factors.

1. **Net present worth rule:** This is for computing the current estimation of your net future incomes from real estate interests. To calculate the projected revenues' net present value, you have to discount all future revenues by the ideal return rate. Afterward, deduct that value from the underlying money or tour total capital. The standard ideology is that investors should not put resources into a project if the value net present is negative. To calculate net present value: suppose cash flow in a month is $25,000 therefore :

$$\frac{\$25000}{1 + 0.0054} = \$24{,}541.02$$

2. **WACC (weighted average cost of capital) formula:** This measures the debt-risk. It's the weighted average of all money related advances you use when funding an investment. It could also represent all capital expenses (both equity and debt). Investors use the WACC formula to decide the potential risk you could incur during the course of the investment. You ought to be wary of ventures with "loan-to-value" ratios over 75%.
Suppose Higherland ltd. yields a 15% average return and the company's average cost is 5% yearly. Then Higherland ltd. generates a 10% return per dollar investment. Therefore an investor sees Higherland as an investment that would produce 10 cents from every dollar put into it. The value (10-cent) may be used either to pay debts or shared to all shareholders.

3. **Supply and demand:** The value upon which the real estate relies on demand and supply: like regular trade deals, if demand (for the property) is high and the supply is low, costs will increase. Then again, when the supply of properties surpasses demand, prices begin to drop.

Let's assume quantity of supply for some shoes (s)= (-200+50p). and the demand for shoes (d) is = (1000-25p),
therefore: (-200+50p) = (1000-25p)
-75p=1200

4. *Benchmarking:* This is used by investors to estimate whether a property merits the intended investment. Investors have recognized the property's monetary qualities. This refers to the ways by which it can generate income for you, the investor.

The most utilized indicators for benchmark comprise:

- "cash-on-cash" return (the contrast between the yearly income produced and the deposit)
- Debt coverage ratio (if the bond is covered through rent)
- Net income (money left after basic maintenance measures)
- The loan-to-value ratio (the distinction between the balance on bond and the current property value in the market)

For a cash-on-cash (coc) benchmarking example, lets assume:

Down payment = $40,000
Closing costs = $4000
Holding costs = $3000
Up-front repairs = $9000
Total cash invested = $56000

$28,800 – gross rent = $28800
Operating expenses = $11520 (40%)
Net Operating Income = $17280
Financing costs = $9732
Therefore NIAF (Net Income After Financing/Year) is $7,548

NIAF ($7548) ÷ Total Cash Invested ($56000) = coc (13.47%)

Make Plans to Find Deals

The best deals don't simply land in your lap. Discovering values is quite like a treasure hunt. You need to turn more than a handful of stones before you locate a shrouded jewel.

The hunt for real estate deals was a lot simpler a while back. The great Warren Buffett detailed, in a 2016 letter to the shareholders (Berkshire Hathaway) that:

Consistently, foreboding shadows will fill the financial skies, and they will rain gold for a while. When downpours of that sort happen, we must surge outside, conveying washtubs instead of teaspoons.

We ought to consistently have our washtubs prepared for periods when "the rain of gold falls." however, something is said about the other times. During typical financial times, you need to try and make plans to find good deals. What's more, you need to remain restrained with your investment models, so you don't capitulate to the "hot market fever."

Discovering Potential Properties

The clerk's office (For discovering nearby foreclosures): In case you're determined to discover and purchasing foreclosures, visit the website of your county's clerk. You ought to be granted access to property records to discover foreclosures in your general vicinity. If you're lucky enough to find one sufficiently early, you can dive in on a property before the opposition does.

FDIC, HUD, and Fannie Mae (For discovering governmental foreclosures): FDIC (Federal Deposit Insurance Corporation), HUD (housing & urban development), and Fannie Mae all offer online records that:

- Detail foreclosures
- For sale
- Soon-to-be-sold properties.

Remember that you'll need an authorized HUD specialist in case you're hoping to purchase a HUD foreclosure.

RealtyTrac (For discovering bank-owned and real estate owned homes: If you're keen on purchasing owned-assets, RealtyTrac helps with this. The tool lets you discover REO (real estate owned homes), homes owned by banks, and foreclosures throughout the nation. You can even view pre-foreclosures to get in on the early action. Investors can also filter through the city, neighborhood, city, or ZIP code.

MLS service (To access the most properties available): You have to be an authorized agent to get real Multi Listing Service (MLS) information. However, investors can view their public postings through Realtor.com, Trulia, and Zillow. To access more factual information, consider linking with a nearby realtor to get full MLS updates. Simply give them your measures such as city, condition, value range, and so forth. Then request that they set up email notifications when another posting fits.

Auction (For short deals, REOs, foreclosures, etc.): Auction.com lets you look for auction properties the nation over. You can do it on the web, while others are either in a bartering house or a county property's court. This tool also has a portable application that will keep you updated on auctions around you.

Below are some other comparable websites:

- Xome
- RealtyBid
- Hubzu
- Williams and Williams

Assessing Properties and Deciding Worth

Zillow Zestimates (a free tool for gauging prices): If you need a quick estimate of what a property's worth in the prevailing market price, Zillow can help with that. The tool bases its property "Zestimates" on current deals and openly available reports; therefore, it can help you get a picture of how a house would be valued after enhancements. It additionally permits you to look through the latest offered homes in a region to get more profound insights.

Here are more sites that also offer free home estimations:

- Realtor
- Redfin
- Trulia
- Property Shark

CoreLogic's RealQuest (provides nitty-gritty property reports): If you're searching for more nitty-gritty (and likely more exact) valuations, RealQuest can help. It, however, charges a small fee (when you consider what they offer). Request pulls an entire slew of data points for some random location. You'll gain access to records on ownership &

transaction, close by deals, MLS information, assessed property estimations, etc. Investors can also check foreclosure statuses on properties on their radar.

Investability (For assessing a property's performance, financially): The Investability device from Altisource goes past esteeming a property. Among the other things it does it, helps you gauge income, yields, cap rate, and all different monetary outcomes a home can bring. It's particularly focused on single-family real estate investors.

HomeSnap (For mobile assessment of properties): You see a building that you think looks promising while making the rounds? You don't have to keep imagining until you return home. With Homesnap, you can get into the analysis right there, regardless of whether it's for sale or not. Homesnap gives you precise, constant property information just by snapping an image of the property. You can likewise get data like school zones, property history, and so on. You can get the application on either iOS or Android platforms.

The FBI's UCR statistics (For checking crime percentages in the territory): Using the agency's uniform crime reporting (UCR), you'll be able to perceive how safe an environment is before you purchase it? This piece of information serves an important purpose as well. Also, this FBI tool can help. With it, investors can carry-out profound search into the specifics of a random city or network in the U.S. You can search through state, local law enforcement division. You would then filter by entering the type of crime and date to see how safe property is.

FEMA (For deciding if a property is opposed to flooding): With the multiple storms and catastrophic events lately, checking a property's flood hazard is reasonable. Simply head over to FEMA's website (Federal Emergency Management Agency) and enter the location of the property you're thinking about purchasing. You'll see an intuitive flood map showing you the flood risks in the area.

GreatSchools (For neighborhood school evaluations): Why is this important? The school quality of the locality is a significant factor when you're showcasing to families. Through GreatSchools, you can assess school locale evaluations just as individual grounds scores and surveys. There's even information on test scores, understudy progress, educators, discipline records, and that's just the beginning.

Below are more resources for measuring school quality:

- The state's education organization
- Neighborhoodscout.com
- National center for education statistics (NCES)
- Niche.com

AreaVibes (To check crime rates, scores on livability, and so on): Need a more profound image of a property? This site covers education and crime like the websites above, yet besides, it tosses in evaluations concerning employability, weather, home affordability, living cost, and amenities. This information is also available on local demographics.

Google Maps (To view a distant but potential property): If you're considering making investments into a property outside your neighborhood, Maps can help you assess it. Regardless of where you reside and the potential real estate. First, type in the location then opens the street to view the property's natural form. In case you need to check out the area.

Financing Your Properties

The following is a list of resources to help you deal with finances before you begin the real estate investment:

AnnualCreditReport (To help check your credit before you apply for a loan): Each American is qualified for a free yearly credit report from every one of the three credit departments (Equifax, TransUnion, and Experian). Try to pull yours before beginning any investment, as it can give you a clearer image of your credit and your financing alternatives.

Credit Repair: Ways to help yourself out (To fix-up your credit when it's needed): When your credit isn't adequate, the FTC (Federal Trade Commission) has a few hints for improving it. The department provides resources for spotting real credit fix programs and evading scams. You can checkout Experian and FICO for additional tips on improving your credit as well.

Freddie Mac and Fannie Mae credit for real estate investments (For a cheap payment contract): In certain situations, it's possible to utilize the Freddie Mac & Fannie Mae installment advances to fund your investment property. Smart real Estate has a strong breakdown of what this involves and how to know if you're qualified. You can likewise check out loan programs available on both agencies (Freddie's Home Possible and Fannie's Home ready).

Flipping and Renovation

Thumbtack (For finding legitimate contractors): Fixing and flipping a house? Except if you're a DIY genius, you'll need some assistance en route. With Thumbtack, you can look for verified temporary workers and rebuilding specialists in your locality and view audits, evaluations, and other information. You can search by type of project in case you don't know which specialist is needed for a job.

Below are other sites to discover temporary workers:

- Home depot
- The directory of the NAHB (National Association of Home Builders)
- Houzz
- Angie's List
- HomeAdvisor
- Porch

FHA 203(k) Renovation Loans (loans to help your renovations):

Need assistance taking care of the expenses of your renovations? The 203k contract credit from the Federal Housing Administration is simply directed to such purposes. It's for single-family properties, and there are cutoff points to what (and how much) the credit can cover.

In any case, it could make your fix-and-flip dreams a reality. Ensure you go through the FHA-authorized lender in case you're keen on utilizing one.

The technique to Quickly Estimating a Property's ARV (For the real estate you intend to fix and flip): Considering fixing and flipping a home? This nitty-gritty manual can assist you in assessing the property after fix value. Made by long-term contributing coach, Mr. Chad Carson. In the guide, he explains the 3-step procedure is easy, and you can do this process again for any potential property you're interested in

RehabValuator (For simple fix-and-flip deals assessments): Intended for flippers and rehabbers, RehabValuator encourages you to figure right-size offers, dissect possible deals calculate the renovation expenses and results. You can likewise utilize it to control your activities and financial plans too.

Property Rental and Management

RocketLawyer (For making your rental application): Rocket-Lawyer encourages you to make state-explicit rent applications with a couple of snaps. Answer a couple of inquiries regarding your property and ideal rental plan, hit submit, and download or print your application immediately. You can likewise download other valuable, authoritative records like past-due notification, credit references request, and the likes.

RentMarketplace (For screening expected inhabitants): Rent-Marketplace smoothes out the whole procedure for prospecting. Use it to make your rental application, run credit and historical verifications on expected inhabitants, and execute your rent with the selected renter. It even offers highlights past the rent payment processing if you're searching for a long term deal.

Below are other tools for screening occupants:

- E-renter
- Zumper
- Mysmartmove
- Experian
- Rentprep
- Myrental

NOLO (For making your leases and agreements): This notable hub for everything legitimate provides an assortment of private rent arrangements for procurement. Likewise, you can purchase rent end contracts and many other landowners and occupant-related structures on the site.

Rentometer (For deciding reasonable market lease): Need to know what a property could get on the current rental market? Head to Rentometer.com and enter a couple of insights concerning the home. In a split second, you'll observe normal practically identical rents for the area just as where your proposed lease falls on.

Also, Altisource's RentRange is another great tool when setting your lease.

RentTrack (For gathering rent): Need to guarantee quick payment of lease installments every month? Use RentTrack. It provides payment processing through the internet and also reports those installments to credit departments. This permits occupants to build credit and lift their scores simultaneously.

Below are other tools like this:

- Rentec Direct
- Schedule my Rent
- Sparkrental
- Rentsy

- Avail

Cozy (For dealing with the property (and the books): This is one of the most popular real estate equipment right now. It helps with everything from market your properties and screen renters to oversee expenses and speak with occupants. Some of Cozy is free; however, parts like screening reports, estimates, etc. do not come for free.

Below are other property management solutions to incorporate:

- Entrate
- Yardi Breeze
- Tenant cloud
- Appfolio
- Buildium

Angie's List (discover property management agencies that offer help): Do you need to lease your properties but don't have any desire to do all the grimy work? You can now employ a property management agency to help with activities to expand productivity. They help with fixes, gather lease, and manage tenants for your sake. All investors will have to do is collect money. Check the property management agents working in your vicinity by heading to Angie's List.

Filter by state or city to make your search more specific.

Quickbooks (For book-keeping): Quickbooks are the best regarding bookkeeping programming; it's actually still in use by millions around the world. They have a cloud-based version as well as that of the desktop. This tool can also be synced with your bank to make the following costs overly simple.

There are also other tools that carry-out similar functions, like:

- Bench
- Wave
- Xero
- Freshbooks

The real estate market is very investment-attractive. Specialists believe that the industry can only continue to grow as it has already recorded an increase in investments of $689 billion in 2018. Simultaneously, real estate remains an unfamiliar zone for technological projects.

A lot of people generally view it as somewhat traditionalist. You can say that this sector is typically inert to advancement. Individuals just couldn't envision purchasing a building without involving either an agent or a broker. However, more and more tools and resources are being produced now.

Change is forever constant, and now digital methods are getting involved in the business. We often see digital innovations improving real estate in the last couple of years. Finally, we're witnessing the change in real estate's conservative image, and everyone in this game now understands that the new technologies will bring new life into the industry.

How about we study the way one can purchase a house, for instance. Homebuyers now have quite a number of ways to shop for a home: There are apps, physical visits, or sires. The internet simplifies the pursuit by a preselected standard.

A buyer can now compare houses and, accordingly, pick the best one. This happens even before the buyer meets with a realtor. Thus, a realtor serves the purpose of an intermediary between the purchaser and the house/land. However, he has no direct influence on the decision, permitting the purchaser to pick.

Let's check out the probable acts of a potential buyer?

- ✓ He/she does the search for the house with a cell phone
- ✓ He/she viewed the sites where different purchasers share their experience
- ✓ He/she connects with the agent and checks on about 10 houses before selecting the house

What features of a website will you find useful as a real estate buyer?

- ✓ Images of several houses
- ✓ Well detailed information on the house, its luxuries, and features
- ✓ Interactive guides
- ✓ Virtual tour of the house

For instance, the digitalization of the real estate market is effectively taking shape in Thailand. This creates new open doors for investors in the country; however, there are a few local real estate issues. Analysts find that 9 out of 10 new organizations shut down the same year they opened.

Fundamental explanations for the failure

- ✓ Lack of understanding of market needs (49%).
- ✓ Lack of investment (29%)
- ✓ Poor collaboration (29%).

New companies, made by people without accomplices, are frequently shut because of poor marketing and cooperation. Specialists note: A major ingredient to going into 10% of effective new companies is understanding market needs.

New real estate organizations ought to begin with reconsidering the everyday issues. Here technology ought to make the lives of purchasers, homeowners, and other market members easier.

Also, there's an opportunity for the advanced land stages to democratize the market where domain operators had previously. By making a commercial center for purchasers and dealers, computerized land stages may help keep domain specialists fair, commission charges lower and land more cash in the customer's pockets.

Some portion of computerized advancements is equipped towards the millennial age, who should set up a business in a hurry and routinely move around the nation. Twenty to thirty-year-olds ha condos for lease a lot of thoughts. Numerous youthful recent college grads, for instance, put resources into green property.

In recent years, you can review just a single I.T. fire up that accomplished genuine outcomes here — it's Airbnb, a notable stage for transient rental lodging. There are only no other similarly effective worldwide parts in the business section or long haul leasing.

Is there any sense in dispatching land tasks or beginning a land profession? Do you know what specialties are the most encouraging at this point?

What Plans of Action are Available?

Classic

The classic real estate model is the resource that gathers ads, assembled by their familiar attributes.

This model showed up at the beginning of the Internet when clients looked for lodging on gatherings and classifieds in the nineties—taking advantage of these resources than did not come cheap.

Paid-to-access-content services

A few projects generate income through paid content. For instance, the sites that help people find lofts for lease and reserve full admittance to their information base to just paid users. The fact here is only a few of these sites actually offer information that you can't find somewhere else for free.

Services for agents

One of the well-known real estate models is the creation of agent-specific platforms such as the ad aggregator websites. Such platforms make life simpler for real estate agents who need to place advertisements on the greatest networks available to discover buyers or renters.

Real estate organizations on the internet

These websites distribute great photographs of the properties. They also enable clients to view the pictures either through phone apps or on the web. This is more helpful than working with the offline agents, and accordingly, this plan of action is very encouraging. These organizations bring in cash similarly to conventional ones. However, they earn through commissions.

Service Models

The ideology here is that the company provides many services. This helps to complete the loft during the whole term of the rent. The owner can pick out the maintenance bundles, which incorporate free inhabitant screening, cleaning the condo, cosmetic repairs, utility payments, and insurance. A monthly rent-charge of 5-10% is discounted.

If you are ready to begin your real estate investment journey, always remember that building a real estate company is always a profitable venture. The market still has a lot of opportunities left unutilized. The market is changing: powerless players are going, new fascinating organizations are developing. The race between pioneers is getting more extreme. The primary issue is that the innovations are changing and improving very fast; therefore, you need to be fluid, moving with the times.

To begin, you need to:

- Consider the situation of the real market

Rivalry in the industry's customary niches is at an all-time high, and no one but pioneers can get a sufficiently high income. The organizations occupying "3-4-5" spots in their specialty are earning very little money.

Pick a promising model for your business.

However, there are numerous monetizing options: the one that seems most encouraging presently is the "service" model. Organizations acquaint innovations with their various tasks.

Consider entering the international market.

As part of the business model, Pre-lay is about scaling and finalizing your model to have no problem when you have to restart somewhere else.

Get a partner

No one knows it all; neither can one person do everything. Getting insight, connections, the essential resources, and financial help from someone who has similar goals is better than what you can learn from any book.

Chapter 2 – Finding Cheap Houses: Off-market Homes

One great way to optimize the return rate of your real estate investment is through off-market properties. However, new investors in the industry are often at a disadvantage as they have no idea where to discover properties except through MLS.

Here we've compiled a list of 15 ideal ways to discover off-market real estate deals. This will assist you in beginning your real estate journey.

What Is an Off Market Property? The name might sound fancy, but off-market properties simply refer to the real estate that's not recorded on the MLS.

Newbie investors in real estate don't generally understand that to discover properties for sale, you don't need to allude to the Multiple Listing Service. There are numerous approaches to find even better properties with a higher value on the market. An off-market bargain has innumerable benefits. Therefore you should look into this.

Do benefits come with Off-Market properties? Investors should know that off-market properties normally sell for a lot less when compared to MLS postings; why? The dealers who do this don't want to have to pay agent charges; hence they charge a lower cost.

Also, as a buyer, there's less competition for you to face. MLS postings are shown on various websites involved with real estate. As a result, a large number of real estate investors and home traders visit the sites. Hence they can begin contending and outbidding each other immediately.

Another thing about off-market deals is that you gain access to better opportunities when you incorporate it into your investment properties search. Restricting yourself to one system for home sales (for example, MLS postings) denies you of certain opportunities around.

What exactly do we mean by off-Market Real Estate? This alludes to properties that are available on the market, however not in the customary sense. More explicitly, "off-market" refer to the listings that weren't submitted, by brokers, to the MLS or any comparative portals. Off-market trades in this medium are made verbally through the broker's network or the broker himself.

10 methods for discovering Off-Market Properties on the market.

- Driving for dollars
- Auctions on real estate
- Verbally
- Public record
- Wholesalers
- Builders and contractors
- Realtors
- Networking
- Online resources
- Direct mail

Off-market deals can provide various advantages to you as a real estate investor. It can put you in a position where you're in high demand. However, because of their alluring nature, numerous investors are asking how to discover off-market property.

There are various ways to recognize off-market deals, all of which should not be surprising to investors. It is smart to use multiple systems in turn, to guarantee the best outcomes. For those who are ready, here are some great strategies to find off-market real estate deals.

1. *Marketing through direct mails*

One of the most proficient approaches to discover off-market deals is via this means. Characterize your target home dealer and send the seller postcards or different promotions that express your enthusiasm for buying their home. At times, mortgage holders don't realize they are prepared to sell until they are given an appealing offer.

Before executing this procedure, ensure that you do your homework and the fact that you should investigate the qualities of the group you're targeting and take note of the best way to communicate with them.

You can pick from either postcard, yellow letters, or even transport seat adverts; the modes are unending. When executing this standard mail system, know that you will not get results immediately.

Try not to get disheartened when you get yourself planning more than one regular postal mail crusade without something positive. Always remember this; this is the best off-market strategy.

2. *Online Resources*

While online sites like Zillow and Trulia principally include properties recorded on the MLS, they can sometimes be utilized to discover off-market bargains. How? Take Zillow, for instance: Zillow permits vendors to list their properties 30 days before the property is recorded on the MLS. To exploit this, investors should follow these locales consistently with the goal that they remain in front of the opposition.

There are likewise various sites that offer off-market postings. Sites like "Opendoor" guarantee an assortment of advantages for purchasers and merchants; most remarkably, they permit trades in real estate to occur while never recorded on the MLS. Remember that while recognizing properties online is cost-productive, you may have better karma with more proactive lead age procedures. Because of the prominence of the web, even off-market postings included online might be very competitive. With that said, do not preclude this procedure—no one can tell what you may discover.

3. *Networking*

This is the ideal lead generation, and that fact remains constant with off-market properties. You may find that networking gets simpler with time and practice, so don't be reluctant to put yourself out there.

With regard to this method, it's advisable to look for local real estate. You can look at your Facebook, neighborhood REIA (real estate investment association), or announcement boards.

4. *Realtors*

While realtors are generally acquainted with properties on the MLS, they can likewise be similarly as wise regarding finding off-market bargains. To improve your odds of achievement and always be a step ahead of your competition, contact a Realtor who knows about the market you wish to buy in. agents are frequently conscious of which properties will go available.

Investors keen on executing this methodology endeavor to curate a rundown of the top specialists in the market you wish to purchase. You can contact by telephone or email and ask the agent about any off-market listings. Ensure that you have checked their site before you call an agent; frequently, their pocket listings will be classified on the web. Leave your contact data with anybody you address, so they can contact you if need be.

5. *Contractors and builders*

Besides realtors, manufacturers and contractors are great buddies to have if you're hoping to discover great, off-market bargains. Local developers are generally "up to date" about properties where the property holder or investor deserted the work mid venture due to finances.

While this circumstance is lamentable for those selling, it tends to be a win situation for investors who are prepared to dip in, finish the work, and make money at closing. This is why having contractors can go a long way in making you more money. Simply maintain total honesty all through your networking. Tell them that you are an investor searching for off-market properties. Thusly, you will start to gain their trust and regard for other realtors in your market.

6. *Wholesalers*

Wholesalers are incredible companions to have as an investor searching for off-market properties. Why? Since wholesalers have some expertise in that: land wholesaling.

At its center, wholesaling comprises finding a limited property, putting it under the agreement, allocating the agreement to purchasers, and charging the purchaser an expense. Generally, those limited properties wholesalers find are off-market properties.

Remember, nonetheless, that working with a distributor is as good as working with agents. That means you probably won't get as great a deal if you went directly to the source. Working with wholesalers is a good way to remain on top of your locality's market trends. Keep in mind, regardless if they don't give you openings at the time, they may contact you later on if something nice presents itself.

7. *Public Record*

It is very important to stay on the latest through public records, which regularly includes pre-foreclosures or short deal properties. Those two normally provide lucrative investment openings, and studying papers and local & state government sites help. At times, these sources sometimes mention properties that are going to be listed. That is yet another open door for smart investors.

One tip for finding off-market bargains is to configure alerts on sites like "HUD Home Store," where you'll get notified when nice properties get listed. Furthermore, when studying public records, you may see some listings that have expired. For such occasions, don't be reluctant to contact the seller. All real estate investors need to remain current on all available reports.

8. *Verbally*

Regardless of how you look at it, real estate investing is one business for the people. Anybody close to you should know your identity, your business, and how to get in touch with you. The more you operate through a verbal marketing strategy, the more individuals will consider you when they see an off-market property. This is like the structure of an organization, be that as it may, don't avoid a potential association basically because they are not directly into real estate. No one can tell who will lead you to your next best deal.

9. Auctions on real estate

Auctions are incredible since they generally have a constant flow of off-market properties to browse. To discover auction properties, occasionally peruse potential auction property sites. Try checking Auction.com/ RealtyTrac for leads. Besides perusing the web, you can likewise monitor auctions going on in-country courthouses. Below are the two primary types of auction properties to watch out for:

• Foreclosures: These are maintained separately depending on the district. However, it all usually follows a similar cycle. These properties are regularly sold "with no guarantees" at below the value costs in the market. When searching for foreclosures, accumulate as many details on the property as before choosing to invest resources. Fortunately, all problems can be resolved with a little research before joining the barter.

• Real estate owned (REO): These are properties owned by moneylenders, typically because of an ineffective foreclosure deal. The off-market real estate may be another fresh way to score great deals. Notwithstanding, as an investor, you should try to get these properties reviewed. While banks are probably not going to make changes or fixes that are proper, it is imperative to have the whole picture before offering anything on the property. If you took your time to perform your due diligence, REOs could be an extraordinary off-market opportunity.

When you locate an appealing property, affirm its foreclosure status, area, and offering method. Before appearing at any auction, be certain you've done your examination. Completely research the area and property specs, and set a spending limit for yourself. Doing all these will permit you to remain focused and within your spending plan.

10. Driving For Dollars

Driving through different regions can be fascinating yet powerful to discover off-market properties. As the name recommends, investors have to go looking for deals. The deals you will find the most are either empty or troubled properties, as these will be the simplest off-market homes to spot.

The subsequent step in driving for dollars is to look for the proprietors of empty homes in the county records utilizing the addresses you recorded. Finding the property owner will permit you to connect and ask about the house; once you can obtain any contact data (a telephone number or email), set up a rundown of inquiries to pose. These should help you decide whether you can buy the property and if it's a good deal. While it tends to be tedious, driving for dollars is a completely free system. Contingent upon the zone in which you live, it could be a down to earth approach to look for off-market homes.

5 Benefits of Buying Off-market Homes

As expressed beforehand, there are various reasons that investors might be pulled in to off-market real estate bargains. Below are some of the advantages to consider:

- Reduced Competition For Buyers: Off-market deals give purchasers a major edge because these properties are not open to many different purchasers. Frequently, investors only have to contend with a few other purchasers. This can assist investors with abstaining from bidding-wars or, worst case, losing a good deal.

- Lower Sale Prices: Less rivalry implies that: lower deal prices. Off-market homes aren't broadcasted, and they normally avoid the spotlight. This will allow you to fly under the radar and score properties at an incredible cost before they're even recorded for general society.

- Smooth Negotiations: Because these properties go inconspicuous by most, the purchasers and sellers are more comfortable when negotiations begin. This can prompt the sort of agreements that could never be conceivable on the open market.

- Adjustable Transaction Times: In real estate off-market deals, you will probably find that vendors are not in any hurry. As a buyer, this permits you to take as much time as is needed before making an offer. It's essential to note that specific deals, like, pre-foreclosures and short deals, may require a more rapid closing measure.

- Unique Opportunities: The explanation behind some off-market land postings can be because of miserable conditions in the dealer's interest. There might be a monetary issue or an owner hoping to make a brisk (and calm) exit from the property. These circumstances can be commonly helpful for both parties, offering alluring agreement advantages and overall revenues for them.

Summary

In general, real estate off-market deals can offer multiple advantages for all investors who make the right moves. By providing less rivalry and adaptable dealings, off-market land can help investors earn overall revenues. Although it's not on the MLS, there are various strategies for everyone who learns how to discover off-market bargains. It advisable for investors to use multiple techniques (along with the ones explained here) in turn. You can add new deals to your portfolio, and off-market real estate should not be an exception.

Chapter 3 – Best Places to Buy Cheap Land, How Much Those Property Costs and Price Range

Whenever there's a boom in the real estate market, the buyers will seek to purchase practically any house that enters the market. While it lasts, it's a great feeling. However, when the good times have come and gone, homebuyers who pick the best areas alone will own the most important properties, which devalues at a slower rate. The location of a property is the value difference in real estate.

Like you must have heard, real estate is truly about "location, location, location." This is a solid counsel, only that most individuals have no clue what it truly implies.

The right location can mean various things to various individuals. However, there are additional factors that decide the value of a house. Contingent on your own very needs, you will most likely be unable to purchase a home with all these components. That's OK because, after all, houses are substantially more than investments. Be that as it may, whenever you're looking for another property, remember the following factors:

1. Centrality

Where you decide to live in a city or town will, without a doubt, influence the amount you pay for your home. The land is limited, so urban areas like San Francisco that are well developed and don't have much space for additional development, will in general, cost more than urban communities yet to develop. A portion of these places has an enormous number of uninhabited homes and territories that have fallen into decay.

This endless suburbia happens a lot because of populace development, as indicated by the U.S. Department of Census Data (Urbanized Areas). When rambling urban communities experience mass departure, it's the peripheral territories that will suffer most in property value. That's how location affects the principal economic tenets of demand & supply.

2. Neighborhood

The areas that appeal to you normally involve individual interest. Be that as it may, a great neighborhood will share a couple of key variables like availability, appearance, and comforts. Your community may likewise determine the size of your home.

Regarding accessibility, you should search for a local located close to the city's primary travel routes and has more than one point of the passage. Driving to and from work is major in the lives of numerous individuals. So a house with easy access to the streets and transportation will be more attractive than concealed.

The look of the area is also significant. Huge trees, beautiful landscapes, and close-by parks or community centers are typically attractive. You can likewise tell how popular the site is by the duration the homes spend on the market; if turnover is speedy, you're by all account not the only one who thinks this is an attractive spot to live.

A proper neighborhood ought to comprise amenities, like, cafes, shops, and markets. Many people like to visit places that are comfortable or lively. If you need to drive a significant stretch to get to anything, your home is likely not so appealing.

Schools are another significant enhancement. Regardless of whether you don't have children, so long as you need to sell your home, later on, numerous purchasers will be watching out for good schools. The nature of nearby schools and the good ways from the house are both significant variables to consider.

At last, remember safety. A local known for less crime but inviting and safe to be outside to mix with neighbors is the kind of place everyone wants to call home.

3. Development

It isn't only the current amenities that count; future ones matter too. Things such as plans for new clinics, schools, public transportation, and other community frameworks can significantly improve property estimations in the region. Business advancement also raises the value of a property when you're looking for a home, an attempt to see if any new businesses or private advancements are arranged and consider how these increments may influence the allure of your potential location.

Having a property close to a community center, school, hospital, or fire station can bring down its worth due to traffic and clamor.

4. Lot Location

Consider where the house is. In this case, there are a few issues you should remember as you execute your search.

If the house you plan to is directly on a bustling street or close to an expressway, you can presumably get it at a lower cost; however, selling it will be hard later. The same goes for houses close to or back onto the business property, for example, a market or corner store, or houses on roads that get lots of parking traffic, or even those close to popular places of worship or public venues.

Then again, a house with a brilliant view or near a waterway is probably going to be well valued, both now and when it comes time to sell it.

5. The House Itself

There's one part of house-hunting that shocks individuals. Suppose you've limited your options to two homes that stand one next to the other in an incredible neighborhood. One needs fixes and renovation but has a huge buy lot. The other is very fit as a fiddle; however, it sits on a lot of large proportions. Suppose the costs of the two homes are the same. Which do you pick? Much of the time, the house needing fixes is the better option.

The explanation: your home is a devaluing asset. The lot, then again, will keep up its worth (or even appreciate). Let's say you decided to destroy the two houses; the bigger lot would sell better. Thus, if you're stuck in such situations you can, pick a greater, better-molded, or better-located lot over a more pleasant house.

A less charming house can generally be renovated, redesigned, or supplanted, yet the lot can't be changed.

Location is not subjective; actually, it depends on a static kind of rules. When a person goes home-shopping, he should ensure the area isn't only alluring to him that it has characteristics, like safe roads, appealing amenities, and good schools. All these will help guarantee your investment increases in value with time.

When the conversation is "buying a cheap property," one needs to consider the "catch" Ever since the U.S. economy-crash in the 2007-2008 Global Financial Crisis, we've noticed a consistent increment in the costs of land. Before you consider purchasing real estate or land, you have to comprehend what makes land modest or more costly than other commodities in the market. When you hear realtors singing "location," there's a motivation behind it. For instance, you'll find empty land at a more reasonable cost in the market because of the nonexistence of structures, schools, medical clinics, power or water lines, and more.

In today's wildlife reality, these terrains have an income-producing potential because of specific grounds that cut to wildlife. Consequently, they are somewhat expensive in the market. Here is a list of U.S. States that you can find Cheap Land to buy

Many lands states are as modest as possible in the U.S.; the principal reasons are generally the condition and the area of these terrains. Sometimes these lands need accommodation, people, and amenities, giving investors more concerns for loneliness alongside maintenance issues.

Although they may really be cheap on paper, they're very costly when you consider driving to and from urban communities to get the pleasantries, renovations works, maintenance, building, reestablishing ranches, etc.

Most of these cheap terrains are made for investors who'd favor constructing their building from the earliest stage or basically fixing and flipping certain properties to sell later.

- Kansas

When prices are being discussed, Marquette, Kansas, ought to be at the head of any list. They are right now offering land so modest, and it's essentially free. Many land deals are occurring in a portion of the towns here. Cons: You'll discover more open and empty spaces instead of buildings and individuals. You'll essentially find numerous little tight-knit communities here. To be a proprietor of such a modest land, you'll need to construct your house from scratch and live there for a year to guarantee full possession.

- Maine

In Maine (Camden), 24 persons get employed in the town after a five-year interval, allowing them to provide 2.8 acres of land to any individual who comes to town to do business. The city is available for both residential and commercial development. Cons: You'll be required to pay an upfront installment of $175,000, which will be discounted once you get acknowledged for their payroll and satisfy every one of their prerequisites.

- Oregon

If you're among those individuals who are a tremendous fanatic of waterfront properties, you should look at Oregon. There are many wild terrains, particularly in the North Bend area, close to the Adventure Coast. That part is especially picking up and gaining recognition from investors.

The terrains at Oregon are truly near urban communities, subsequently making amenities more effectively accessible. There is additionally plenty of empty landscapes available for those who'd favor being just 3 hours from Seattle, close to the sea. You can also enjoy the view of some game real estate.

- Louisiana

Hoping to claim your very own farm with some sensible prices range in the market? Look no further; Louisiana is your smartest choice. Cons: The main con is, a portion of the territories in Louisiana are generally off the map. Thus, don't anticipate finding ripe soil, appropriately working water system frameworks, or grand square fields. These terrains will require attention, care, and time to get your farmland looking as you imagined it to be.

If you were pondering in terms of cheap ranches, the best place to check would be Idaho. The issues with farms are, they must be in an ideal spot where the land ought to be sufficiently enormous. This will lead to open spaces for the domesticated animals; for instance, grazing area, wellsprings of water, and close-by amenities; this is why it's generally hard to discover ranches as modest as farmlands.

In any case, at present, you can discover ranches available to be purchased in Idaho at sensible prices if you check the right places.

- Detroit

It's fundamentally a buyer's heaven in Detroit. There's plenty of sellers who are happy to offer reasonable prices on deals and houses. Many of the homes are truly near shopping malls and cafés, making driving to and from simpler. Cons: You can wager there's something fishy going on here, particularly when you can get a 4,800 square-foot house for $500. The explanation is a significant number of the homes in some parts are deteriorating and will require a long time to swim out of the wreck they're in. Or then again, the house itself is in critical condition that it'll require a ton of affection, upkeep, fixing, and time.

- Nevada

Are you searching for raw and cheap land? Gerlach, Nevada, takes this to another level entirely. Here the terrains are as modest as $157 per section of land. Cons: These terrains are just plain old lands. They have practically no vegetation, they're hot as Hades (thanks to the desserts), and wherever you look, you can basically observe distant fields. Seek to get these terrains at modest prices for every section of land and get them in mass.

When looking at the least expensive spots to purchase land in the U.S., focus your sights toward the country's Southwestern side. Where there are states like Western Kansas, Texas, Colorado, Arizona, Utah, Nevada, California, Washington, Idaho, and Oregon. Toward the Northeast of Florida, we have Jacksonville, an ideal place for empty terrains and has loads of possibilities, particularly for those hoping to build a property from the beginning. At times, a considerable lot of the barren landscapes are sought after by the investors.

With empty terrains, since you have a fresh start, you get the opportunity to choose how you'd like to manage the land. Also, when you see a ton of potential in a land, it simply improves. For instance, the forest area in Arizona or Oregon is one of the best locations for investors to get into the farming industry or purchase a lodge to appreciate.

Timberlands are a portion of the land market's prime properties, all due to their lovely and pleasant landscapes. When purchasing, note that your property will cost per acre. Therefore, you have to investigate each part of the land you are attempting to invest in. Verify whether it's an ideal area for cultivating or housing, making the property more costly than the others. For instance, there are some farmlands available in Washington that are quite expensive.

They're going to be costly because these grounds have enormous regions of thick prolific soil, the absolute best grazing zones for animals, well-arranged water system frameworks, houses and lodges, offices, and a great deal of luxuries close-by. Make sure to look at little pockets of land nearer to the urban areas, similar to Chattanooga (Tennessee), Buffalo (New York), Tampa Bay (Florida).

Presently, online land deals are where a significant number of these lands are being sold like hotcakes, particularly when you're in your house and can get to investigate real estate on the web or through satellite imagery.

Risk and Techniques When Thinking About Online Land Sales

Before you proceed to check-out those listings online, there are some things you'll need to evaluate before taking the dive. For example, you'll need to decide what you intend to do with the land you're going to put resources into. Would you say you are getting it to build up a house, school, a ranch, and so forth?

Do you plan on getting it first, afterward fixing and flipping it, or do you want to make a residence for you and your family to live in, or would you say you are anticipating leasing it out? After you've chosen what you'd prefer to do, the cycle doesn't stop there. When you see a land property online that sparks your interest, check and review a portion of the property's subtleties, area, size, shape, etc.

Before signing the check, you should get onto the site and investigate the property. More often than not, what it resembles on paper, isn't what you'll generally get. Verify the land quality if it's tainted by asbestos or another synthetic or if the ground is sufficiently strong to set down establishments that won't break or break down later on.

Access to amenities and utilities is the main consideration to consider when purchasing a property. You'll need to ensure that there are passages to public regions, for example, schools, cafés, malls, and so on. Also, be aware of the zoning limitations on your potential property. For example, the floor area ration, the stature of the structure you intend to construct, the lot. Also, know the facilities for accessories (like carports, pool houses, and so on). When purchasing empty & crude land, remember that you'll build up the property from the ground up. This implies that there'll be plenty of costs to consider, particularly since nothing isn't anything income to be expected.

Along these lines, you'll be leaving a great deal of cash tied up into a property, with taxes, upkeep, and purchasing the property. The golden rule to purchasing any property is to pose inquiries and a ton of them so that in the end, you don't make a painful decision.

When it comes down to purchasing real estate in the U.S., be it on the web or real life, ensure you do your examination, locate the correct area, converse with suitable individuals. Also, talk about your real estate skills before you settle on your choice. After all, you'll be contributing your time, energy, and cash into a land that could provide you with immense incomes. Ensure the property you pick suits you and your family.

Cheap U.S Lands for Retirees to Invest In

In case you're a current or prospective retiree, you're presumably searching for innovative ways to support your savings and increase future salary. Numerous individuals decide to put their resources in rental properties. However, that venture comes with stressful duties, including consistent calls from irritating tenants about broken faucets and noisy door hinges. This is definitely why some people are going into vacant land investment.

Known as land –speculation, buying empty land for potential future profit is a high-risk venture. The idea is to discover modest land in underdeveloped zones that could boom in the near future. While picking the correct spot can be dubious, you could offer your territory to real estate agents to handle it for you, but also, you could do what they'll do for you, so why lose money?

If this is a venture, you might consider, here are five U.S. states where you can purchase very good land, where your investment may yield dividends for you.

Tennessee

This landlocked state is generally acclaimed for its capital, Nashville. The core of the country-music scene is the Grand Ole Opry's home, the Country Music Hall of Fame, alongside an incredible stretch of honky-tonks and ballrooms. Memphis, situated in southwest Tennessee, is another area where vacationers run to see "Elvis Presley's Graceland." In eastern Tennessee, the Great Smoky Mountains, located along the North Carolina fringe, offer a tranquil region to fish, climb, and take in lofty mountain sees. Tennessee additionally offers another significant favorable position—no state salary charge.

Indeed, even with varying attractions, land in Tennessee is generally reasonable. For example, in Unicoi County, situated in the state's precipitous upper east, the sum of the normal deal for a 251,911 square foot is $59,408. That is just $0.37 per square foot. As Tennessee keeps on developing, you might benefit from a land buy in the Volunteer State.

Arkansas

Called the Natural State, Arkansas outskirts the Mississippi River and is notable for its wealth of outdoor entertainment from hunting, fishing, mountain biking, and hiking. The state's topography incorporates mountains, thick woods, swamps, lakes, waterways, supplies, and streams.

Arkansas likewise has a minimal living cost, a developing economy, and a mounting populace. The least expensive land in the Natural State can be found in Clay County, settled in the upper east corner of Arkansas, where land sells for around $0.07 per square foot, with the normal deal cost of only $43,083 for an 830,617 square foot part.

West Virginia

Arranged totally in the Appalachian district, it's no big surprise West Virginia is known as the Mountain State—the landscape is uneven. Harpers Ferry, situated in the upper east of the state where the Shenandoah River meets the Potomac, is a famous vacationer site. The site of the acclaimed pre-Civil War attack by John Brown is encircled by a noteworthy public park, with a significant number of the structures open to general society as relic galleries.

West Virginia's economy is as yet developing. The biggest business in the Mountain State is still coal mining, representing 98% of West Virginia's development. You can, at present, discover pleasant land in West Virginia. In Morgan County, which is simply an hour outside of Harpers Ferry, a square foot of empty land will cost you around $0.44. With a normal parcel size of 277,623 square feet, that goes for $29,450.

New Mexico

Here is the Land of Enchantment, New Mexico boasts a cluster of striking scenes, like the Chihuahuan Desert, "Sangre de Cristo Mountains." The southwestern state's capital, Santa Fe, is a mainstream vacationer location notable for its upscale spas, sublime Spanish provincial design, and dynamic social scene. This flourishing city is home to the "Georgia O'Keeffe Museum" and the Santa Fe Opera.

To finish it off, New Mexico's populace and economy are on the ascent. As such, the Land of Enchantment could likewise be the place where there are new chances at life for retirees hoping to purchase multiple vacant lands. In Quay County, the earth goes for about $1.96 per square foot, and the normal land deal sum is $55,918.

Arizona

Most popular for its never-ending sunny climate and, obviously, the Grand Canyon, Arizona has, for some time, been a tourist attraction for vacationers desiring a sample of the southwest. It's additionally the 6th biggest state in the U.S. with a quickly rising populace. Arizona's occupation market is very solid when contrasted with numerous different states.

Indeed, even with those numbers, you can, in any case, score modest land in the Grand Canyon State. In Santa Cruz County, situated in southern Arizona along the Mexico outskirt, the normal cost of land is $1.77, with a normal deals measure of $45,420 for 91,088 square feet.

Regardless of whether you end up discovering bargain-basement land in one of these five states, recollect that any land buy is a big risk. Particularly for newbie real estate investors. Before you buy a plot of land, cautiously consider the territory's development projection. Also, consider all drafting necessities, geology, and expense commitments related to possessing the land. Also, ensure it has water and easy access to utilities.

Regardless of whether you're thinking about purchasing a current home or buying a plot of land on which to fabricate another house, the two choices require impressive exploration. The two alternatives additionally have some significant contrasts you ought to know about so as to make an educated choice.

Differences between Building a House and Buying Land for Building a House

Among the differences between the two is how loans are organized. Home loans/mortgages arrive in a scope of alternatives to suit your requirements and financial plan. However, there are fewer options for buying land. Many land credits must be completely paid from three to five years.

Interests and upfront payments are likewise higher when it comes to land loans than for mortgages. A normal advance can go from 20% to 50%. Although, a few banks will demand a little less in advance payments if you have a fantastic credit score.

One of the advantages of buying land with money is that the sum you pay for the land can be utilized as an initial installment towards your development advance when you're prepared to begin constructing the house. Sometimes moneylenders can likewise add your land-buy with the construction loan.

Most specialists suggest buying the land with money if you have it. Real estate agents can help show you your options. Also, a financial advisor can help you in selling resources or orchestrating money moves.

Why you should consider purchasing Land

In numerous regions, present housing markets are somewhat very competitive. New homes are being bought before they're even completed. Older houses come with long-standing issues. If the current markets do not offer what you need, buying land and having your own home worked to your details might be a more lucrative move.

Purchasing lands allows you more opportunity and less interruption from close-by neighbors and expensive HOAs. If you're purchasing your private land, it's presumably a proper decision for you.

Things to consider when buying land

You'll have to sort out your financial plans to permit the acquisition of lands and home construction. Besides development costs, you'll likewise need to consider extra expenses, including charges, licenses, and land adjustments. If necessary, and the expense of running water, utility, sewers to the home. The advice of a real estate specialist is crucial here.

Ways to Find Land to purchase when you want to Build a Home

When you're looking for land to buy, try to get in touch with a certified rural land specialist instead of a residential realtor. Without experience in land trades, a realtor can wind up either wasting your precious time, cash, or even both. First, look for a certified agent around you, or you can peruse the properties recorded under a qualified agent.

Make sure to question your agents before agreeing to do business with them.

The need for a Qualified Land Agent before Buying Land

A certified agent has the experience and knowledge to boost your territory exchange value. The agents will be able to give you the necessary assets, information that a customary realtor would not disclose to you. Also, you'll be able to save a lot of money since they're very much aware of the costs, administrative work, and legalities of buying land. Below are some other things a certified land agent can help you in the business:

- They'll have details about the zoning laws enumerating what should and should not be done on the land you wish to buy.

- They have important information regarding the city statutes you would need to follow.

- They can assist you with recruiting an expert surveyor should you need one.

- They can help you assess the utility expenses for running water and electricity to your new home.

- They know about easements.

- They can inform you concerning the lot you mean to buy as regards the floodplain.

- They can assist you with licenses before you begin developing your home.

Chapter 4 – Investing in Real Estate with Little Money

Real estate is an incredible investment with many numerous advantages. When you purchase a real estate investment, money comes in from various places such as salary, devaluation, appreciation, equity build-up, and influence.

Furthermore, real estate investing is a crossbreed between an independent venture and pure investment. While it's not so simple, you can start the business and grow it from the ground up.

Once your business develops, you'll be able to enjoy the benefits of your investment. This also implies that work becomes optional, and you can do whatever you work whenever you want.

15 Ways You Can Invest in Real Estate, Spending Little Money

House Hacking

This is one of the strongest ways to begin your real estate investment journey. It fundamentally requires you to find ways to create rental money through your house.

One classic house hack is for you to move into a little multi-unit building, similar to a triplex, duplex, and 4-plex. Afterward, you will lease the additional units for the money.

As an investor, you should also get imaginative by leasing additional rooms to flatmates, leasing a cellar loft or visitor house, or additional rooms on your parcel to an R.V. (as long as your area's laws permit it).

You can kick-start all this with minimal capital since you can get "owner-occupying" money to purchase the property. Here are a couple of projects with small initial payments that you can access to begin your house hacking:

- 3.5% (down) FHA (federal housing administration) loan. A person with 580 in credit score easily qualifies for this loan.

- 0% (down for veterans) VA (The veterans affairs) loan program has numerous requirements. Below are some of this:

    - ✓ A minimum of 90 days consecutively spent serving in wartime
    - ✓ A minimum of 181 days of service during peacetime
    - ✓ Six years service with the US national guard/reserves

- 0% (down in rural regions) USDA (the US department of agriculture) loan program offers different plans for different people. You can visit their website to know the requirements.

- 3% - 10% (mortgage insurance) These are conventional loans like the one you get from banks, credit unions and more.

Starting with a property worth $200,000, for instance, you may put about $0 - $7,000 with a few of those programs.

Master Leases (Leasing Options)

Do you realize that you don't have to purchase a house to begin investing in real estate? Rather, you can lease it.

Master leasing is where you lease a property and get authorization from the proprietor to sublease the additional rooms or units to different occupants.

For instance, suppose you lease a 3-room apartment for $1,500(monthly). Then you discover two flatmates who each pay $600(monthly), which is $1,200(monthly). Your share from this plan is just $300 every month (when you find the difference in $1,500 – $1,200).

Furthermore, as with most rentals, this plan can regularly be negotiated with almost no forthright cash. Maybe a security store, prepaid lease, or a proposal to do a few fixes.

And keeping in mind that simply ace renting may be adequate now and again, you can likewise attempt to arrange what's called an alternative to buy. This gives you the option to purchase the property at a set cost during a specific timeframe.

For instance, you may arrange an alternative cost of $175,000 for an apartment in the earlier model for 3 years. If the price rises to $200,000, you would be able to purchase the property to hold it. You may even flip to sell to another person.

Live-In House Flip

This is probably the ideal method to begin with, flipping. This strategy is known as the "Live-In Flip." It exploits one of the most beneficial tax laws in America.

To start this model, you have to purchase a home, reside there for a minimum of 2 out of 5 years. Afterward, you can profitably sell the house without paying taxes (up to $250,000 as one person or $500,000 as a couple).

Right there is one major no-tax profit. How long would you need to work to bring in that much cash pre-tax?

Similar to each methodology, it doesn't come without some hustle and danger. But since you live in the house, you can decrease the risk by taking as much time as is needed with fixes, and then you wait for the right time.

The strategy (reduced down-payment) would work perfectly for Live-In Flips. Many people have utilized Live-In House Flips to construct a few hundred thousand dollars of total assets right off the bat in their working vocations. Then they developed this savings into $2 million, which permitted them to stop working in their 40s.

Live-In-Then-Rent

This strategy is quite similar to house hacking. Basically, you move into a house, prepare it to lease, and afterward keep it as a rental later on when you move out.

To make this methodology work, you'll have to purchase a more modest house that will likewise work financially as a rental.

Similar to house hacking, you can profit by the little initial owner-inhabitants loans. However, dissimilar to a house hack, you don't need to live nearby to your occupants!

Furthermore, the house is just a little greater than a condo, making this strategy more valuable to individuals with families.

With just 3 or 4 Live-In-Then-Rent houses, you can create a decent portfolio for a long time.

Crowdfunding in real estate

Crowdfunding in real estate is a moderately new technique in the real estate industry. It permits you to contribute a more modest measure of cash (like $1,000 to $5,000) together with a gathering of different investors in the group.

These crowdfunded ventures could be on rentals (normally bigger multi-unit properties) or credit to the other investors.

This method has been tested numerous for years. But since the legitimate structure and organizations are so new, people are still somewhat careful.

For instance, let's say a colleague had some cash with an organization called Realtystocks, and they essentially stopped working a year ago. Money has not been lost yet, but it shows the danger of investing with new businesses that are broken.

So this implies that while some investors like the general idea, there is still speculation to a moderate level of their total assets until further notice.

Some of the companies to check include:

- Peer Street – Loans for other investors with about 7-8% in interest

- Equity Multiple & Crowdstreet – Business projects (pre-vetted) or trade projects that have diversified portfolios

In these cases, you have to be a certified investor to contribute. This implies you'll need to have assets surpassing 1 million dollars (apart from your home). Also, you need to be earning a yearly salary of over $200,000 (or $300,000 for a couple).

REITs (Real Estate Investment Trusts)

REITs (real estate investment trusts) are fundamentally the same as mutual funds. When you purchase stock in a REIT, you own a share in numerous business and income-generating properties. A group of supervisors selects and manages the investments inside the REIT.

Like crowdfunding, REITs are passive once you get it. However, unlike crowdfunding, portions of a REIT are substantially more liquid (meaning you can sell them rapidly like stock or shared asset) to raise money.

Airbnb

Airbnb is the online commercial center that lets you lease your home (or part of it) for brief time frames. Yes, you can also use it as a vehicle to get into the real estate business.

Most people consistently lodge in Airbnb condos when traveling, especially those who love having their own kitchen and space.

For the vast majority of you, this system could be a specific type of house hacking as you generate income from your home. In any case, you could likewise develop it into a real business that creates low maintenance or full-time pay.

Partnership

When you don't have the capital yourself for real estate, you can begin with a partner's money.

Although there are numerous methods for partnership in real estate, one of the least complex is something many refer to as a "credit partnership." It fundamentally works this way:

- You locate a decent real estate deal.
- Your partner sets you up with the necessary funds to purchase the property.
- You rent the property from your partner with a clause that allows you to buy it at a greater cost.
- You sublease the property to a tenant. You handle all the everyday issues and keep what's left from the lease you gather and the lease you pay.
- Before your buy-back option expires, you can get another loan to buy the property (ideally after the property has gained value). Or rather, you could offer the interest you earn from the property to another purchaser at an increased fee.

With careful thinking and hard work to assemble a deal, you can basically control the salary and the energy about the property with almost no cash (maybe a token of $100 to $1,000 in option fees expense).

Seller Financing

Seller financing is a way that involves buying real estate in a place where the merchant can "become the bank" for you. Rather than getting an advance from a bank, the seller lets you buy the property after some time through a monthly payment plan.

This is a decent way to purchase real estate because conventional bank loaning requirements don't limit these people. The terms you and the seller agree on is what you pay.

It's not the norm, but it sometimes happens that you negotiate a lesser down-payment with your seller. This particularly works when a property needs fixes as you can exchange your labor (sweat equity) rather than making an upfront installment.

BRRRR Strategy

This represents Buy, Remodel, Rent, Refinance, Repeat. Like flipping, it's quite centered on discovering fixer-upper houses, rebuilding them, and expanding their worth. Be that as it may, rather than selling, you keep the property as a rental and renegotiate to pull out a few or the entirety of your money.

This arrangement is most helpful when you're attempting to develop your rental portfolio rather rapidly. Rather than running out of money for forthright expenses on numerous properties, you can cautiously renegotiate to pull out your money. The money can then be reused to purchase a few properties in succession.

The following explains how the cycle works:

- B – Buy a house with the potential to rise in value after fixes. You'll typically use purchase financings, such as credit extension, cash, hard money, or private money.

- R – Remodel it to build its worth and make it rentable

- R – Rent it out to the right occupant (or inhabitants)

- R – Refinance through a mortgage (long-term)

- R – Repeat

This is a strategy that numerous investors have practiced this for a while and made good profits through it.

- *Carefully borrow your down-payment*

This is one of those procedures to consider with little excitement because borrowing capital is not really ideal.

However, if you do it cautiously and take care of the assets rapidly, it could help you begin your journey into real estate success.

For instance, if you have access to the HELOC (home equity line of credit), you could make money on your home's value for an up-front installment or the whole acquisition of the property. Afterward, you can devise a plan to rapidly payback from property generated income or from the savings.

Also, investors could be allowed to access as much as $50,000 out of the 401k assets. However, you should be ready to pay interest to yourself. You should also repay the cash in a sensible timeframe. However, paying yourself is better than paying a bank.

- Become a realtor

To start this, you could begin a side business or full-time profession as a realtor. This is not investing in the real essence, but it's an incredible method to learn how the real estate market works.

Each state is somewhat unique, yet you normally need to take some classes in advance (about 30 hours in South Carolina). Afterward, you can sit for a comprehensive study and pay up your licensing obligations with the state.

Furthermore, you'll need to locate a broker's office to "hang your license" with. There is a wide range of firms and diversified models, so you'll need to find the one that works for you.

Lastly, most operators normally join their local association of Realtors and pay for access to the MLS.

Your initial investment would range from $1,000 to $2,000. In any case, you'll have to put extra time and energy into marketing to begin earning through income.

- Be a Bird Dog (find Deals For Others)

To legitimately make money as a finder, you must be with your real estate license. Thus, this is a specific type of realtor work. However, rather than zeroing in on all purchasers, you center around buyers who are an investor.

This technique is quite basic and simple to follow. You simply need to complete two things perfectly:

1. Discover great deals

2. Discover numerous investor buyers with money. It is advisable to check out your local REIA groups for investor buyers.

- Wholesaling

Wholesaling is the matter of discovering limited deals and rapidly reselling them to earn money for other bargain hunters. Much of the time, with little capital, anyone can benefit from a wholesale bargain.

Wholesalers and deal finders have very little differences. You get the property under an agreement or get it before you trade it for money with wholesaling. However, as a bird-dog, your investor purchaser is the person to who you sell the property.

Wholesaling isn't the ideal amateur plan of action that people sometimes think it is, but anyone can work this out carefully and make money.

The issue is that wholesaling is a business. This implies you must be okay with making offers to people and getting dismissed a LOT.

- Discover Tenants For Rental people

If you later need to learn to be a rental proprietor yet don't have the money, consider turning into a renting agent to bring in money while learning the business.

To do this, your job is to help link an occupant with a specific rental unit. What's more, you will get a fee (usually between 50% to 100% of a month's lease) in return for your time.

This strategy is great for future rental proprietors since you'll be learning how to discover and screen tenants, which is one of the fundamental abilities to be a landowner. Also, you do it while bringing in cash and having little risk on your part.

Most times, you would be working for a management organization before you become good at the business. Be that as it may, investors could get your license and contact singular landowners and offer your services as well.

Rental proprietors need this service, so you're sure to find people who are willing to work with you as long as you're good.

Now that you've learned 15 separate ways to begin investing in real estate With Little Money let's answer some of the frequently asked questions people ask.

Can I purchase Property Without any up-front payment?

Yes, It is possible to do that. To purchase a property with no advance payment, you'll need to have access to the right financing.

For instance, VA loans (the loan meant for military veterans or dynamic individuals) come with a 0% initial installment. What's more, a US Department of Agriculture advance has a 0% upfront installment for properties in qualified regions.

Certain people have purchased or controlled properties for no-down-payment with imaginative financing techniques, similar to rent options, seller financing, and credit partnerships.

Also, BRRRR is probably the most mainstream type of investing (without money). It's a favorite among investors because this method helps build your property's value and brings down risk. This means you pull out most or the entirety of your up-front installment by refinancing.

Would I be able to Invest in Real Estate without Money and with a Bad Credit?

Most investors begin their investment journeys with difficult money related circumstances. Maybe you have minimal expenditure spared, and you have awful credit from a past budgetary test. If this is the case, you have two choices, to begin with.

You can begin on a full-time or part-time basis like a realtor, bird-dogging, leasing agent, or wholesaling. These options are all great choices, so long as you earn while you learn.

As a future real estate investor, you can likewise use innovative financing techniques to purchase or control. Since you're not seeking a loan, any merchant or private person might be more tolerant of credit. These methodologies incorporate lease options, master leasing, seller financing, credit partnerships, hard money, and private money.

While these choices are conceivable, remember that saving and repairing your credit should be utmost in your mind. Make it your objective to not need to be in a position to invest with terrible credit.

Chapter 5 – Flipping: The Strategy for Continuous Real Estate Profits

Flipping houses is about purchasing a property, holding it for some time, then selling it, with the mind of making money. Rather than buying the home as your resident, you're purchasing it as an investment.

At times, flipping implies that the impermanent owner will be required to make many renovations and fixes. At other times and on different occasions, flipping has to do with keeping the property until you can sell it for more money (in addition to whatever amount you spent while renovating it).

The objective is to purchase low and sell high, contribute your labor value to reduce expenses and make a profit within a short period of time (normally ranging from months to a year).

Upsides and Downsides of Flipping a House

A real estate investor named Matt Aitchison makes so much money flipping houses, and now, he is busy telling other people the best way to do it (and earning extra income from that).

Coupled with several different businesses, Mr. Aitchison manages the 6 Figure Flipper, a platform that shows individuals how to flip houses. No matter how much you make, he believes certain other benefits (and hazards) are involved in house flipping.

The Pros

• It could make you a nice profit in specific business sectors: By 2019 second quarter, the profit from a normal house-flip was $62,700, as per a report published in ATTOM Data Solutions. Aitchison discloses that he makes about $40,000-$50,000 per flip. The most he's acquired from a house flip was $453,000. However, that is an extraordinary anomaly. A realtor can assist you with exploring projections regarding price growth.

That will help you discover locales and homes that will provide you with the highest return on investment.

• Side hustle/new job: The money here totally depends on you, as you could earn a lot or meager, contingent upon the number of flips you take on. While the additional time you put into it can result in more income, you don't have to work more than you need to. A few persons start house-flipping and inevitably move into it full-time. Others use it as an optional stream of income to earn more to save more, go on vacation, or as their retirement fund.

However, if you do flipping as a side hustle, don't take on more than you can deal with.

• Helps you increase neighborhood values: When you flip homes, you contribute to the increase in your area's value. Aitchison stated that the vast majority of the houses he purchases are in a troubled condition or originating from a troubled dealer. It's an extra motivation to get into flipping when you realize that you can take care of somebody's problem while making good money for yourself.

The Cons

• Risks: The vulnerability involved with house flipping may result in loss of money, thereby leading to health problems. Flipping can be monetarily depleting, and this tends to be when you don't have the correct partnership, attitude, and discipline.

• The houses will probably have huge problems: Generally, home flippers need to put huge amounts of money into repairing the homes they purchase to flip them. Additionally, you probably will need to spend a lot more to remodel if unexpected problems emerge. For instance, imagine a scenario where you discover asbestos on your property or Termites? Or Mold? The risks are many and could be costly. The worst case is when you find out that the reparations you need to exceed the budget.

• Potential for legitimate issues: If you purchase a home that doesn't have a clear title or sell it and it has problems you didn't fix or address suitably, you'll always have to deal with the consistent threat of a lawsuit. That is the reason for having a strong team to support you is significant.

• The property probably won't sell rapidly: When a house that you're attempting to flip sites for long on the market, you'll have to continually pay expenses such as mortgage payment (if you're on financing), home-owners insurance, and property taxes. Remember the potential home-owners dues and maintenance levies. Thus, it's significant that you have some capital saved up for all possible outcomes.

Step by Step Instructions to Begin House Flipping

So long as you're aware that flipping homes aren't a thing you can begin overnight, it's pertinent to ensure that your funds are arranged and the correct properties.

Set a financial plan: A major drain is when an investor does not have enough capital to finish a task that he's undertaken. Try not to go in moderately; It's advisable to increase your present budget times five because whatever you believe is sufficient most likely isn't particularly if this is your first time.

Find the right property: If you don't have an enormous budget, search for properties that best fit your current income. Peruse through sales, foreclosures, and short deals to see which ones match your current account for remodeling. Look out for a real estate agent (if necessary) who has experienced working with flippers.

Make offers: With the proper finance and correct property, you can make an offer. Work with an agent that can assist in maintaining your spending plan. It's OK if a request fails to work out; you can focus on having numerous properties if it doesn't work out.

Plan a timeline: Not every renovation demands the same capital, which implies they don't need a similar timeframe. Whether it's one month or six, give yourself sufficient time to make the suitable fixes and redesigns, and factor as expected for building reviews.

Hire contractors you can trust: Except you have what you need to deal with fixes and redesigns yourself, you'll need to employ respectable individuals to accomplish the fundamental work.

Quite a number of workers have full teams trained and experienced in handling all areas of home renovation. Check licenses and references for temporary workers you need to employ, and ensure their fees are well within the capacity of your budget. Also, ensure that they meet deadlines.

Sell the property: After the fixes, it's time to put your property on the market to be purchased. While you could sell it yourself, a realtor can help you promote the home to the correct purchasers. Keep in mind that the agents know the market and the property's potential value. Therefore they can be priceless when it's time to sell.

Common House-flipping Errors New Investors Make

Although there is a ton of money to be made from house flipping, however, some basic misstep house flippers normally make. Some of these are:

• Insufficient capital: It's the venture you want to get into that decides the budget, and very few homes are well renovated. Some properties are full home redesigns, which means you can tidy up and sell. That only requires essential fixes, which you would then be able to put available for the investors. Whatever your budget is, double it twice, afterward add your initial account, and then you're ready to start. Everything could get messy very easily when you don't know what you're doing. Worst case scenario, the contractors will exploit you if they figure out you're a newbie.

• Thinking it's simple: Although no one needs a license to begin flipping homes, it's by no means a get-rich-quick scheme. Companions or TV shows should deceive nobody. Flipping requires lots of money and patience, and no investor should go in blindfolded.

• Inability to get the right team together: As an investor, it's pertinent you work with reputable and experienced individuals. Endeavor to find an accomplished house flipping tutor, a realtor, rebuilding/construction company, real estate lawyer, home inspector, and a bookkeeper to assist you.

• Doing it as a long-term side hustle: It is the belief of many that a house flipper business will be 10 times more difficult if you still work a 9 to 5. Who's going to be at the site if you're working all day and an issue comes up? Flipping isn't ideal as a part-time business; if you must, do it full time.

Financing

Before you start flipping, see to it that your finances are prepared. There are lots of home advances you can acquire capital from. Personal loans are accessible for home-related fixes. However, analyze the financing costs and loan terms first before you do anything.

As a beginner, know that the odds are stacked against you as far as this business is concerned: as expected, energy and capital are vital. Save yourself from despair by keeping strong crisis-investment funds in case of emergency. Many seasoned real estate investors believe that house-flipping should be practiced as a side-hustle. However, you might want to begin as such before getting into it full-time. That way, you have your normal employment salary when and if the market turns on you.

Know the Market

A number of house flippers get pumped-up about the next venture and typically overlook the importance of really knowing the business. All potential investors should know that if they don't have a decent comprehension of the market and strong vicinity patterns, problems will arise. Investors should be properly prepared for whenever they may run into any of the issues below:

- You don't have a clue whether you're being offered a proper deal on the house you're purchasing. The selling price should be sufficiently low, so you will have any money to perform the renovations and still make a profit in the end.

- You can't precisely tell the potential value of the property. Your vision for the house has to align with the reality in the locality. Also, the local's inhabitants' capacity to manage the cost of the home you're about to make must be considered.

- You have no idea how to negotiate the price of the house. If you've purchased a house in an area of generally $130–150K homes, you'll need to value your flip at the lower side of that range whenever it's the opportunity to sell comes.

So how would you acquire the market knowledge that makes for a successful flip? It would help if you located a real estate agent who has had years of business experience. Who also understands the territory you intend to flip in. The agent can assist you by focusing your property search on the correct neighborhoods dependent on your value point, budget, and expected profit.

Beginner investors might look at a house they discovered online and think it's a great deal at $145,000 and has heaps of potential. However, if the most delightful and biggest house in the area sold for $160,000 3 months back, any remodels would presumably out-price the area, leaving you with a home you'll be unable to sell.

It's better to work with a realtor who understands the market in and out. When you're prepared to sell, with the agent's insight, he'll be able to value the house properly, helping you to rake in as much profit as possible. Having a "rock star realtor" on your side can help you make profitable investments that will keep the dollar flowing in your direction.

Make a Budget for Your House Flip

No sensible investor waits till after he/she has purchased a property before he/she decides to devise a budget. Know your value range for:

- Buying a home
- Making fixes
- Finishing renovations

- Paying the selling costs before sealing any deals.

Create a rundown of any cosmetics tasks and/or any costly overhauls like pipes or electrical issues. If you don't know about construction, a contractual worker can disclose all the things to be fixed and the amount it will cost. Un-expected fixes can break a flipping venture. Therefore make certain to do your due diligence on this part.

When you're under the agreement, make sure you secure a home inspector's services to inspect your property fully. It's ideal to see a problem and prepare for it before it surprises you.

Spend resources on Smart Renovations

Fantasies about glimmering hardwood floors, trending installations, astounding kitchens, complete with "professional-grade ovens" can rapidly make your redesigns a success. That is the reason it's critical to know your financial plan in advance and afterward ensure your renovations remain on track.

Remember that enormous renovations such as restrooms and kitchens can represent the deciding factor in your flip. For instance, renovating the kitchen, as indicated in "2020 Cost versus value report", the normal sum spent on a significant kitchen rebuild is nearly $68,500. The normal sum recovered from that cost is about $40,000. Now, that's not the sort of "return of investment" any investor desires from a house flip.

In case you're redesigning a house that you would like to sell for $220,000, do not spend $60,000 on "custom cabinet installations", top-of-the-line finishes and a "fantasy kitchen island". Rather, consider a more astute redesign that centers on refining the current cupboards, including granite counters and supplanting worn-out appliances. You'll spend less and have a much higher probability of gaining back your costs when you exchange the house.

As you execute your renovation investments, don't think little of the so-called little tweaks. Things such as a new layer of paint, fresh landscaping and an updated hardware can have an immense effect!

Seek the guidance of a Real Estate Guru in your area

Would house flipping be profitable for you? YES when done the correct way. In 2019, the average price of flipped houses was almost $218,000 with profit edging towards $63,000.

Remember that the gross benefit does exclude the sum spent on fixes and redesigns. Yet, in case you're ready to flip with money and remain in your budget, it's very possible to make an extraordinary profit from your venture.

The way to flipping a house effectively is to, make a shrewd investment in the kind of house you buy, pick renovations within the budget, and sell it fast. To achieve all this, you'll need to have a realtor in your corner.

Regardless of whether you're purchasing a house to live in for a long time or to flip in a half year, a quality realtor can give the market information and handy direction you need to thrive in this business.

7 Indications of a Bombed Flip

The following are seven indications of a bombed flip, according to the gurus in real estate.

1. New flooring flaws

To get a quick appraisal of the general nature of a flip, simply peer down at the floor. Saltzman believes that poor workmanship on new deck is an admonition sign.

The best possible strategy is to eliminate the base trim and remove the bottoms of the doorjambs and lay your flooring underneath.

Saltzman considers a flawed flooring as a frequent indicator of more genuine defects including the electrical work and plumbing.

2. Imprudent workmanship on the kitchen

Everybody realizes that kitchens sell homes. However, it's believed that a gleaming, stainless steel machines and "granite countertops" can't conceal a useless format.

Holes among backsplash, ledges and fresh doors ineffectively introduced on old cupboards also represent poor workmanship.

Once things aren't assembled well, they will self-destruct rapidly. In any case, Saltzman is more worried by things he can't immediately see. A piece of good advice to new investors is, "try not to be occupied by the kitchen bling."

3. An electrical wiring that shocks

Given the present-day codes for safety, can you take shortcuts as a home-flippers with the electrical framework?

Saltzman says that people certainly do. Individuals do their own wiring, not knowing how to do it to code. Also, this sort of people frequently have an excessive number of lights or outlets on a solitary circuit.

As an investor, despise the laziness that comes from ineffectively positioned light switches and confined, out of reach outlets. Mostly those have to do with outlining and choices that were made after the outlining went up.

There are codes to forestall the likely risks that a house and its occupants may encounter. Despite the fact that it can run over $10,000 to rework a house, that is one part where corners ought to never be cut.

4. Doors that don't work appropriately

One regular makeover error may be disregarded on an easygoing stroll through. However, be careful with the inside or outside doors that:

- Do not shut smoothly
- Fail to hook securely
- Tend to either close or open by themselves

A similar issue can skew windows, as well.

Whether it's through climate or the house finishing itself, after you've finished a lot of work on it, things can move by millimeters, thereby prompting the house to not work too.

The issue additionally can be as a result of a typical contractor shortcut: supplanting the door yet not the current jamb.

A rushed or messy work can wreak havoc as well. So what solution do we offer?

If you're really serious about doing the right thing, grab a level along with you and fix it on both the doorjambs and door to check whether they square up.

5. Mismatched metals

Being an expert interior architect, Karu realizes how to blend metallic finishes on lighting, faucets, door handles and cabinet pulls.

This should be done carefully in view of a plan. An investor would definitely see that the metals are not equal, but rather it would look right and fitting, and the completions are not modest.

Lamentably, house flippers are famous for picking cost over appearance.

Most times, what you find in a flip is, individuals could get equipment at a bargain and lighting discounted as well as plumbing installations on sale; however, none of it matches. In any case, the investors couldn't care less since it was totally bought on sale.

You should know that deceiving with bling has its drawback and that is; when individuals simply toss costly installations in there that aren't fitted right, then it would appear that you're concealing something.

6. The HVAC (Heating Ventilating and Air Conditioning) framework gets harmed during construction

A perfectly working HVAC, warming, or ventilating & cooling system is the core of a comfy home.

Tragically, when a house-flipping group transforms a home into a development zone for maybe months, the harm that drywall dust and the likes can do to your home's HVAC system is terrible.

You can go to the "furnace blower fan" and place your finger across any of the blower fan edges to check whether it's covered in drywall dust. If it is, then the evaporator center of the air system will most likely be covered in drywall residue. You'll need to have the entirety of this expertly cleaned.

7. Unsafe safety features

Flippers can be nervy with regards to safety rails and the other features of safety present in the home they've gained.

Safety features are certainly managed by code, however, code goes to the underlying establishment of something. If something was constructed following the code at the time it was done, then it'll still meet code today. Although it might not meet the code of another installment.

The outcomes can be risky. Saltzman (an Auditor) has seen flippers reattach security handrails into only drywall!

Karu states that all house flippers have both a financial and moral responsibility to make safe home flips.

As a flipper, you're liable for keeping up the security of a house; that is the thing that codes are for. It must be protected on the grounds that you're responsible (for at least a year) for the security of individuals living in the home you're flipping.

As to whether purchasing & holding real estate or flipping is the better investment doesn't have one right answer. Rather, picking one technique over the other ought to be the vital part of your plan.

You ought to likewise consider the chances presented by the current market. Below is a quick view into the things to consider if you want to go with "buy-and-hold. This should help you to decide which is ideal for you.

The Pros and Cons of Buy-and-Hold

Pros

- ✓ Taxes
- ✓ Ongoing income
- ✓ Increasing property value

Cons

- ✓ Vacancy costs
- ✓ Legal & management issues

Pro: Taxes

With investment properties, you have tax advantages that aren't possible with flipping. Rentals are taxed just like investment income, having a lesser tax rate. You can likewise discount costs, including fixes, support or upkeep, paying a property administrator, and driving back and forth from your property.

Besides, you'll be taxed at long-term capital gains rate if you choose to sell subsequent to possessing the property for over a year.

Pro: Ongoing income

Possessing investment property gives you standard pay, regardless of where you are or what you are doing. Furthermore, purchasing and holding land is a known formula for gathering incredible riches. In spite of times of diminishing prices, the value of land always seems to bounce back over the long haul because there is limited land supply.

Pro: Increasing Property Value

The more you hold the property, then almost certainly, you will profit by expansion. That will support the property's estimation while the sum you obtained for the home loan goes down as you take care of it

There's additionally a real potential for big profit if you were able to buy your property during a buyer's market and make sale during a seller's market.

Con: Vacancy Costs

Not being able to discover inhabitants is one of the dangers of possessing rental property. This is a major issue regardless if you do it without anyone else's help or recruit a management organization. If your property sits void for quite a long time or years, you are liable for covering the home loan during that period. Prior to putting resources into a purchase-and-hold property, you'll need to ensure your capital covers at least 1 – 3 months of vacancy per year.

Con: Management and Legal Issues

Long-term proprietorship in real estate is one serious "management-intensive" business that's quite outside the range of an investor's abilities. A few financial specialists, particularly first-time proprietors, are usually unprepared to manage the obligations and legal issues that accompany being a landowner. The procedures to discovering quality occupants and addressing their necessities can be a distressing and time-consuming endeavor.

Picking a Strategy

You have to address a couple of basic inquiries to choose whether flipping properties or holding them is the best for you. You should know if your real estate capital allocation can last long or simply an approach to benefit from an ascent in home costs.

It will help if you figured out the "risk and return ratio" is proper for this section in your portfolio. Lastly, you should already possess the danger-tolerance skills to execute the administrative duties that accompany either investment.

Assume the capital isn't accessible to buy an expanded portfolio. Then, a potential investor must be ready to take on "unsystematic risk". This incorporates singular property dangers and a possible absence of interest for the property.

You can appreciate the two methodologies' advantages by building up your business flipping houses then utilizing the profits to put start-off long-term rental properties.

Chapter 6 – How to Use Online Resources; The Social Media Tool

Although businesses of all sizes and shapes can profit from a savvy social media presence, the significance of this tool in real estate truly couldn't be more important.

As indicated by a new report from the "National Association of Realtors" social media is now fundamental to acquiring customers and snagging bargains all through the market. The following is a concise depiction of the report's discoveries:

- 77 percent of real estate professionals effectively utilize web-based media for real estate in some way.

- 47 percent of real estate organizations disclose that socials generate the greatest leads.

- 99 percent of recent college grads and another 90% of "baby boomers" start their search for home on the web.

Interpretation? socials is a flat out goldmine for real estate investors. Obviously, that is supposing you have a solid social methodology and aren't simply blindly going for it.

Regardless of whether you're beginning without any preparation or need to sort out some way to win more leads, we have you secured with our manual for social media for investors.

Real Estate Marketing Toolkit

Once you're into real estate, then you must be really occupied. You have to organize your time and concentrate on the online media platforms that serve your purpose.

In view of the noted study above, Facebook has 97%, LinkedIn has 59% and Instagram has 39%. These are the top picks for realtors.

Facebook for real estate professionals

Facebook is an easy decision and is still a major advertising tool for realtors. A central explanation behind this is that Facebook's client socioeconomics speak to the target group for all realtors regardless of the business age and expected income.

Past being the place your crowd is likely hanging out, the business highlights incorporated with Facebook are ideal for real estate investors.

For instance, Facebook permits organizations to share listing-related posts, book arrangements, speak with clients and also curate reviews all in one place.

LinkedIn for real estate professionals

As a basically B2B (Business to Business) organization, LinkedIn isn't really some place to spot customers.

In any case, it is a phenomenal spot to connect with individual real estate agents as well as display your experience.

Instagram for real estate professionals

This is a real boomer for anyone into real estate at the present time and the reason is a no-brainer. Upscale property photographs go inseparably well with the most well-known types of Instagram content. For extravagance or boutique real estate plans, Instagram is increasingly becoming a priority, rather than just an "auxiliary" social tool.

Moreover, features, like, the "Instagram Story" make it a snap for real estate professionals to give brisk and customized property updates daily.

Essentially, the market for real estate is formally on the web. What used to be an industry that relied upon cold pitching and customary promoting, is currently an industry that depends intensely on online media showcasing.

Any real estate professional now should be able to see how enormous an effect, social media has on building trust in your customer base. This is a significant lead generator for realtors, yet most land brands neglect to expand their effectiveness on the web.

It's easy to change your content system so as to accomplish extraordinary outcomes for your brand. Here are some hints:

1. Utilize the Right Real Estate Hashtags to Optimize Your Content

Hashtags are regularly misconstrued as a strategy with the sole reason to build "likes" on a social media post. While hashtags do carry greater commitment to your content, they additionally lead to discovery on socials. This is a straight road to gaining potential clients.

You can utilize land hashtags for your content, as a superb path to meeting purchasers and homeowners. However, hashtags are a stunningly better route for you to find likely purchasers and open doors for your real estate business.

The following are some hashtags you can use to discover likely homebuyers or to draw in potential real estate customers:

Nonexclusive Real Estate Hashtags

#homelisting #oldhousecharm #justlisted #renovated #justlisted #broker #forsale #homesale #newhome #househunting #dreamhome #properties #property #homesforsale #openhouse #homeinspection #homesweethome #foreclosure #reo #realestate #realtor #fixandfliphouses #homeevaluation #housing #mortgage

Realtor Hashtags

#realestatebroker #propertyforsale #businessbrokerage #commercialrealestate #commercialboardofrealtors #realestateagent #realestatelife #homebuyer #realestateinvestment #business #realtoroffice #banking #invest #investmentsales #realestate #listingagent #homebuyers

Personalized Real Estate Hashtags

#[Brokerage Name] #[Target City]property #[Real Estate Team Name] #[Target Neighbourhood] #[Target City]homes

Since Instagram permits 30 hashtags (maximum) for each comment or caption, there are 30 hashtags for you to use for a more broad real estate Instagram posts. You can also do some watchword research and pick hashtags that are more pertinent to your brand.

Use Hashtag Tools

If your hashtags aren't creating the commitment you'd like, there are some incredible hashtag apparatuses accessible to assist you with solving this issue. Hashtagify is a mainstream device that makes recommendations for "Twitter hashtags". It also permits you to follow and examine the hashtags.

Ritetag provides hashtag proposals for pictures or text on any site, based on constant engagement information. The two platforms provide free trials of their services, in case you're uncertain they'll be worth the cost.

2. Add Realtor Quotes to Your Content

If you maintain a real estate venture, you'd probably know how troublesome it can be to devise a real content. You're searching for witty ideas that reverberate with your crowd, so you can zero in your primary endeavors on purchasing or selling homes.

Quotes on real estate as well as testimonials are incredible additions to incorporate. The fun and effusive nature of sharing quotes can assist you with building trust and brotherhood with your crowd.

You can likewise contact past clients and check whether they are happy to give any personal testimonials. With these, you would then be able to utilize instruments like Snappa to transform these testimonials into web-based media designs for your showcasing needs.

3. Use only the Best Social Media Tools

Time is consistently a scant asset, so augmenting productivity is significant in online real estate marketing. There's continually another thing to do, and if you can invest less time making content, you can invest additional time closing in on deals and purchasing homes.

There are lots of real estate marketing apps that can help to save time, increase exposure to buyers and vice versa. The people at G2Crowd.com have made a matrix to look at a portion of the diverse real estate products in the business.

With the measure of innovation and assets accessible online today, you can streamline and computerize your marketing.

10 Hints That Will Help You Improve Your Real Estate Advertising

a. Free Stock Photos to help discover Realtor photos

Getting proficient photographs taken can be very costly and despite the fact that it's regularly justified, you might not have the budget for that. Now you can get nice pictures that will function admirably for your online media advertising. There are a lot of sites that offer free stock photographs, yet the absolute best ones include:

- Stocksnap
- Unsplash
- Burst (by Shopify)

b. Making Social Media Graphics for your real estate business

Acquire a decent amount of stock pictures, is a magnificent start for you. In any case, having plenty stock photographs isn't sufficient. You should endeavor to modify your content so that it reverberates with your crowd. With stock photographs, you can make tweaked online media illustrations with text, shapes, and symbols. Now you can make improved content to pass your message to your intended interest group.

Infographics are incredible for engaging with individuals and they give a simple route for your followers to devour your content. In case you're hoping to feature quantitative data, designing a real estate infographic is the best approach! Done effectively, an infographic is a profoundly shareable piece that shows industry ability.

c. Automating your Social Media Marketing Posts

Consistency in your social media posts can have a tremendous effect on your web-based media execution. Having a predictable post plan is basic, however, that can be very hard to execute in the real estate world where your timetable is continually evolving.

That is the reason we propose utilizing free instruments and online assets to assist you with computerizing your posts on socials. That way you can plan content early, and keep to a standard timetable, regardless of whether your timetable is variable.

Tools, like, Hootsuite and Buffer are incredible devices to use to plan your real estate content. Whenever you've wrapped up making your web-based media post, you can incorporate Snappa with Buffer to automate your posts on go.

d. Create Valuable Blog Ideas for your Real Estate

Each real estate site appears to have a blog, however, numerous online journals are either inert or fail to give any genuine incentive to their crowd. Your blog content should demonstrate to your audience your skills in real estate. Also, they have to be advanced to pull into your website new prospects as well as the social handles.

Creating real estate blog ideas may be precarious. However, the following are a few instances of blogging content to improve your real estate advertising:

- Write-ups concerning market forecasts and measurements

- Tips for property holders and what they should understand when purchasing or selling

- Generate posts regarding the area and the general community information

Imagine yourself in the position of a new homeowner that just moved into a new area or those hoping to move into the territory. What information would you be looking for? Odds are another person is pondering something very similar. Blog posts generated in this regard will help acquaint your audience with your skill and brand.

Some great Real Estate Blogs you can model after

To give you an insight into what works for real estate blogs, the following are some decent blogs with huge amounts of traffic.

The BREL (Real Estate Team)

Based out of Toronto, the Brel works admirably with their blog. They work on local content and on data that mortgage holders and home purchasers require. They post their listings week after week with the tag "real estate crush of the week". Giving their readers a superior view of their informative postings.

The group additionally incorporates posts focused on the customer. These posts comprise Q and A sections on different subjects on real estate.

Zillow Blog

Another extraordinary blog on real estate to check out is Zillow. This blog is a real estate commercial center where you can look for listings, analyze home estimations, and communicate with other realtors. Zillow gives extraordinary articles that customers can identify with. Posts loaded up with "what you have to know" or "market trends". This helps to further educate their readers.

e. Optimizing your Real Estate Facebook Ads and Posts for Realtors

Facebook is a broadly utilized platform that property holders and sellers frequently use. Numerous real estate businessmen have had extraordinary achievements through the platform. It is time you took this chance and exploit Facebook to the fullest.

Facebook Posts on Real estate

To begin, you need to have the right Facebook content that wouldn't be boring to your crowd. Also, the posts should be such that can help pull in new leads to your real estate investment. Some mainstream real estate Facebook ideas are:

- Real estate tips on how to purchase and sell homes for newbies
- Showcase the local events and businesses occurring within the community
- Start a challenge or do giveaways to create awareness and generate engagement
- Stories on real estate investors and their testimonials
- Professional pictures and illustrations of new houses available (It's advisable to use a tool like Snappa for this)

What you need to evade is overselling your crowd. Truly, the primary target of your business is to sell homes, however, the social media game is a long-term one. Your crowd will purchase a home when they're prepared so there's no need for pushing a deal when your supporters are not ready to purchase or sell.

Feed your readers with value and awareness with the goal that when the opportunity arrives, your real estate brand will be the primary thing they remember.

Design proper Realtor Ads that will generate better Leads

Facebook is something other than just a social platform for individuals and pages. It offers a huge amount of important information, because of the endless number of clients utilizing the platform. With this information, paying to promote on Facebook is a very savvy move, once done right.

You can focus your advertisement on a group of people in a certain territory with explicit interests. Together with that, you can decide to focus on a crowd of people dependent on their ways of managing money, their family salary, their relationship status. Here you have to get innovative and shape decent Ads to communicate with your readers.

Facebook additionally enables "carousel advertisements", multi-picture promotions which are incredible for realtors. Carousels advertisements permit you to show both the outside and inside of a home. The two can help attract clients as well as give the potential purchaser a fuller image of the various benefits in the house.

f. Share your personal success stories

It might appear as bragging when you post each time you close a deal. However, it really does help your work and build client trust in your real estate brand. The more individuals see you as you purchase and sell, the more they'll believe you when ready to deal with you.

User-generated posts are particularly effective for this situation. Share all individual shout-outs to your page. Also, if your clients are on the net themselves, they can tag you as well to produce a more powerful effect. In any case, endeavor to get a photograph with your cheerful clients in their new home, and post it online.

g. Think about Accessibility

It's not difficult to disregard accessibility when you scarcely have time for social media advertising. However, you cannot afford to forget about accessibility. There are some easy guidelines to follow, and they can propel your advertising to new heights.

As you post your video, remember to add closed captions. They're significant to those who have hearing issues. Know that 85 percent of every Facebook video is viewed while muted. Subtitling the video permits your crowd to burn-through your content however they like.

Picture descriptions shouldn't be extravagant. Simply depict what individuals are seeing so those utilizing screen-readers are in on it as well!

If you're able to provide bilingual services, run promotions in various campaigns in the various dialects you know. Simply try to send them to the applicable presentation pages, with the goal that potential clients will be able to get the message in their preferred language. The key is to make it simple for every individual who needs your services.

h. Incorporate Videos into Your Real Estate Strategy

Videos are incredible alternatives for building a strong rapport with your audience. It's engaging and dynamic, and performs well both in connection and in the algorithms.

Don't be shy about the camera. Always remember to consider the needs of the customer when making your videos. Ensure your recordings offer value to your audience always. Keep your recordings instructive and enlightening and you'll frequently receive huge engagements.

Another mainstream move is "live video". Be comfortable with having to "Go live" constantly as it's an effective way to reach your crowd and drive greater commitment. Live recordings permit you to have a live Q and A meeting, for example, you can do something like "ask me anything about purchasing a home". This should be planned early, so you can share your insights straightforwardly with all potential clients.

i. Work with the Experts and Local Businesses

Numerous real estate professionals have partnerships with other neighborhood businesses, like, home inspectors & stagers, brokers and photographers. It may well be significant to engage with others in your locale, and when you do it's anything but difficult to give each other a lift via web-based media. You can share content among yourselves, and even create it together.

Recall that it's not just about sitting tight for them to share your material. Actually, promoting them can assist you to build a bridge of trust and believability among yourselves.

j. Gather reviews concerning real estate

Nowadays, most employers won't employ until they've perused a couple of reviews. That is the reason it's indispensable that you gather reviews and make it simple for possible clients to access them.

The Reviews tab on Facebook is situated on the left-side, and anyone can send direct links to customers subsequent to working with them. This helps to remind them to give a review.

When a potential client is ready to do business with you, they'll probably first check through your testimonials and reviews. That is the reason having positive reviews directly on your social handles is so significant.

Conclusion

The impact of the social media on marketing has been colossal as regards the world of realtors. The internet has changed the way real estate investors' commune with their customers. Also, it has pushed organizations to be more intelligent and personal with their audiences.

Time is forever an uncommon asset for entrepreneurs and real estate investors are not left out. Setting aside a few minutes for land web-based media marketing can be difficult. However, there are a few instruments and ways for realtors to limit the work and augment results.

By optimizing your ads and content on socials, organizations enjoy better performance which generates profit.

Zero-in on producing content that encompasses your potential customers. When you realize what content to make, utilize as many accessible tools as possible to make lead-generating content. Always consider the position of your customer. What information would be vital to you if you were about to purchase or sell a house? Always feed your clients with value-based content, always, and you will see incredible outcomes.

Chapter 7 – Rental Properties: Where and How to Buy Your First Rental Property

Rewards and income aside, real estate investment can be overwhelming for first-timers. Real estate can be hard and the field is peppered with land mines that can blow-out your profits. That is the reason it's imperative to do a definite exploration before you make the plunge. Rental properties are one of the ways to get into the business with close to no capital, therefore making it a favorite among certain folks. If you want to kick-start this journey, the following are some significant points to note when looking for an income property.

Beginning Your Search

Start the quest for a property by yourself before attempting to involve an expert. An agent may push you to purchase before you have discovered something that suits you. What's more, finding that venture will require some sleuthing aptitudes and a bit of shoe leather.

Doing this exploration will assist you with narrowing down a few key qualities you need for your property like, type, area, amenities and size. Once that is done, then you may need a realtor to assist you with finishing the buy.

Your area choices will be restricted by whether you expect to effectively deal with the property on your own or recruit another person to do it for you. If you mean to effectively oversee it yourself, then don't go for a property that is excessively far from where you live. In a situation whereby you intend to involve a property management agency then proximity is less of an issue.

10 Important Features to Observe

The following is a rundown of 10 features you ought to observe while looking for the proper rental property.

1. Neighborhood

The locale where you purchase will decide the sorts of occupants you'll get as well as the vacancy rate. If you purchase beside a college, odds are that youths will overwhelm your pool of expected occupants. Also, you might have to struggle to fill-up vacancies by spring. Know that certain towns attempt to dissuade rental transformations by imposing excessive grant charges.

2. Property Taxes

This will probably fluctuate throughout your target territory, and it's pertinent you know the amount you'll probably lose. High taxes on property are not generally an awful thing as is the case with beautiful neighborhoods that pull-in long-term occupants. However, there are unappealing areas that additionally have this high rate taxes.

The district's "assessment office" possesses all the tax data on document or you can converse with homeowners in the network. Make certain to see whether property tax increments are forthcoming. A town suffering from financial distress could increase taxes, way past what a landowner can reasonably charge for rent.

3. Schools

Consider the nature of the schools in the locality. Though an investor will be generally worried about the monthly income. If there are nothing but bad schools close by, it can influence the estimation of your venture.

4. Crime

Nobody desires to live near a problematic area of crime. The public library and local police should be able to offer crime statistics that are accurate for neighborhoods. Check the vandalism rates, petty and severe crimes, and remember to note if crime is on the ascent or it's declining. You may need information regarding the police presence in your area.

5. Labor Market

Areas that are improving with employment openings draw in more inhabitants. To discover how a particular region rates for work accessibility, check with the "U.S. Agency of Labor Statistics" Bureau of Labour Statistics (BLS) or visit a locality's public library. If you discover that a major company is about to move to your region, it's certain that laborers looking for shelters will run there. This may make lodging costs go up or down, contingent upon the sort of business included. You can attempt to have that particular company in your terrace as would your tenants.

6. Amenities

Visit the area and look at the parks, eateries, exercise centers, cinemas, road links, and all the various perks that you know might draw in occupants. "City Hall" probably possesses literature that can help you out with the best mix of public conveniences.

7. Future Development

The "municipal planning division" will have data regarding plans or developments that have just been drafted into the territory. In case there's a ton of development going on, it is most likely a proper deal. Watch out for developments which may hurt the cost of local properties. Extra new lodgings would contend with your property.

8. Number of Vacancies & Listings

An area with an uncommonly high rate of listings might flag a seasonal cycle or worse -a declining neighborhood (ensure to discover which it is). In either case, high rates of vacancies drive proprietors to bring down rents to draw in inhabitants; and vice versa

9. Average rents

Since rental money is your "bread-and-butter", therefore you have to know the region's lease on an average. Ensure any property you consider can hold up under lease to cover your home loan installment, charges, and different costs. Explore the area to measure where it's probably going in let's say five years time. In case you can manage the cost presently, however, taxes will probably increase. Therefore today's moderate property could become bankruptcy tomorrow.

10. Natural disasters

Insurance is yet another cost to deduct from your profits, so you have to realize exactly how much it will cost you. If an area is inclined to quakes or flooding, insurance expenses can consume your rental money.

Getting Information

Having an official source to obtain information is great, however, you'll need to converse with the neighbors to acquire the genuine scoop. Converse with both the homeowners and tenants. The tenants will be more honest when divulging the negative details of a neighborhood for obvious reasons. Visit the territory sporadically to see your future neighbors in real life.

Picking a Property

A single-family abode or an apartment suite is usually the two best options for new real estate investors. Condos are typically low maintenance due to the fact that the condo association deals with the exterior fixes, so you only have to stress over the interiors. However, these, will in general generate lesser leases and appreciate slower than single-family houses.

Single-family homes generally draw in longer-term tenants. Families or couples are normally the preferred occupants as opposed to single individuals since they're normally more financially steady.

How to Determine Rent

How can you decide the potential rent? You will need to make an educated guess. Try not to distract/deceive yourself with excessive assumptions. Setting the lease excessively high and winding up with a vacant unit for long can rapidly kill your venture. Start with the normal lease for the area and work from that point. Consider whether your property really merits more pay or less, then find out why.

To sort out if the lease price will work for you, calculate the property's cost. Take away your normal monthly mortgage payment, property charges partitioned by a year, insurance in 12, and a liberal remittance for fixes and maintenance.

Try not to belittle the expenses to keep up the property. These costs rely upon the property's age and how much upkeep you intend to do yourself. A more up to date fabricating most likely will require less work than a more seasoned one. A condo in a retirement network probably would not be dependent upon a similar measure of harm as off-grounds school lodging.

Doing your own fixes reduces expenses significantly, however it likewise implies being available to work all day, whenever there are crises.

Making the Purchase

Banks have harder loaning criteria for rental properties than for main living places. It is their belief that if circumstances get difficult, individuals are less disposed to endanger their homes than a business property. Be ready to pay upfront rates of 20% to 30%, in addition to closing costs. Have the property examined by an expert and also seek the services of a real estate legal advisor before you sign.

Remember to pay for adequate insurance. Tenant's insurance caters for the assets of the inhabitants. However, the structure itself is the proprietor's obligation, and its insurance is costlier than a owner-occupied resident. The interest on the property's home loan, insurance, and devaluation are all "tax-deductible" up to a specific sum.

Each state has great urban areas, each city has it's perks, and each area has great properties. It requires a great deal of footwork and exploration to secure every one of them. When you wind up finding your optimal rental property, keep your desires sensible, and ensure your own funds are sound enough before you begin.

Places You Can Purchase Rental Property

Wondering where to purchase real estate? Actually, the best market for you may not be the best for your colleagues or neighbors. The place where you'll end investing will rely majorly on your objectives.

The best places to purchase an investment property for income and value development, frequently have three things in common:

- Labor development
- Growth of population
- Affordability

When you discover a market that has these three elements, you'll be able to discover decent opportunities for investment.

There are a few urban areas in the United States where these variables exist today — places where you can purchase high-income investment property while costs are still low (around $100,000 as a rule), and watch your value rise.

Below we'll reveal to you 18 of these "best-purchase" markets for rentals investments. Note that these markets are not recorded in a specific order

1. Orlando, Florida

Demand for family (single) homes has been on the ascent in the Sunshine State for a long while. All things considered, it's conceivable to obtain completely redesigned properties in the neighborhoods of Florida for an estimate of $193,000.

More intriguing is that, many people who want to buy homes are deciding to lease rather than purchase. As you can envision, this is making rental rates ascend (over 6% in a year) and this figure is expected to keep rising.

Even with such an incredible income, values are on the rise in these regions with no indication of backing down.

Property insurance & taxes are low, in addition, there's no income tax in the state. Include warm climate and outstanding medical care, and you'll understand why a significant number of the 10,000 children of post-war America are resigning daily to move to Florida.

Orlando is perhaps the best spot for purchasing land and rentals in the territory of Florida. Situated in Florida's "sun belt" locale, Orlando is known for its warm atmosphere, lovely sea shores, world-acclaimed carnivals, amusement, and attractions.

With an ever-increasing population of 2.5 million people (estimated), the real estate market in Orlando is energized by job-hunters, retired baby boomers, and students who need to live in a "modest and merry" region that offers a high caliber lifestyle at a sensible expense.

Market Statistics on Housing

- Average Sales Price - $231000
- Average Month rent - $1486
- Average Household Income - $42418
- Population - 2.6 M
- One Year rate of Job Growth - 3.44 percent
- Seven Year rate of Equity Growth - 110 percent
- Eight Year Population Growth - 30 percent
- Rate of Unemployment - 2.9 percent

Quick Facts on the Housing Market

1. The city is recorded as the number one Best Place to purchase homes by Forbes for the third straight year. Projections recommend up to a 35% expansion in house costs by 2021.

2. Metro Orlando holds the fourth place as the biggest metro zone in the nation, and it's additionally the quickest developing metro in the country.

3. More than 68 million individuals visited the city in 2019. This makes it the most visited tourist center in the U.S.

4. Orlando's populace has grown more than 20% since 2010. Currently, Metro Orlando is home to more than 2.6 million occupants.

5. Rents witnessed development of 3.44% last year. That is 134% higher than the U.S levels.

6. The projected labor growth for the next 10 years is the most noteworthy in America among the two hundred biggest metros according to Forbes.

7. Orlando Medical City flaunts a $7.6 billion monetary effect and will make more than 45,000 employments.

Labor Growth: Orlando's labor force growth is among the best in the U.S. with 45,000 (estimated) new openings made in a year plus a projected development pace of 3.44% yearly for the following ten years.

Growth of population: Orlando's populace has seen an increase of 252% quicker than the public normal in the last 8 years.

Affordability: It is as yet conceivable to buy completely revamped 3-room properties in great neighborhoods for a meager $193,000.

2. Tampa, Florida

Situated on the west bank of Florida, Tampa Bay is a thickly populated metropolitan region (second just to Miami), with a populace of 3 million (estimated) residents. Significant urban areas here incorporate St. Petersburg, Largo, Clearwater, New Port Richey, Holiday and Tampa.

First of all, the economy of the locality is valued at $130 billion (estimated) and the metro zone has been positioned as one of the quickest to develop in America. Tampa additionally puts a solid spotlight on job development in territories, like, money medical care, health care, etc.

Market Statistics on Housing

- Average Sales Price - $225250
- Average Monthly rent - $1485
- Average Household Income - $65196
- Population - 3.1 M
- One Year rate of Job Growth - 2.52 percent
- Seven Year rate of Equity Growth - 106 percent
- Eight Year Population Growth - 12.69 percent
- Rate of Unemployment Rate - 3.4 percent

Quick Facts on the Housing Market

1. The area has more than 3 million people in it, a neighborhood economy valued to be over $130 billion, and is among the most rapidly developing metros in the country.

2. A region with generally costly homes, Tampa actually has pockets for realtors to discover homes at moderate costs (down to even $150,000) then lease for about $1,485 monthly.

3. New Amazon jobs alongside loads of talented residents from the South Florida University helped push the Tampa metropolitan territory to the No. 15 on the Milken Institute's 2018 record of best-performing urban communities.

4. Tampa is home to various Fortune 500 organizations including Publix Super Markets Inc., Jabil Circuit Inc., and WellCare Health Plans, Inc.

5. Tampa maintains its position as a phenomenal tourist center and probably the best city to purchase real estate. It's a mainstream choice for retirees too, accommodating some momentary rental chances.

Occupation Growth: The Tampa metro zone is positioned #15 on the Milken Institute's 2018 record of best-performing urban areas in America.

Populace Growth: The area enjoys a growth of 3.1 million in population, a neighborhood economy valued to be over $130 billion. Also, it's regarded as one of the quickest developing metros inside the country.

Affordability: Tampa has generally extravagant homes, still it has pockets where financial specialists can discover homes at reasonable costs, even as low as $150,000. They can lease them for around $1,485 per month, over the national level.

3. Jacksonville, Florida

Situated on the eastern shore of Florida, Jacksonville lines the two banks of the St. Johns River – the longest waterway in Florida and furthermore one of just two streams in North America that streams north rather than south.

In the previous ten years, this metro region has developed by practically 14%. Till date there are over 1.5 million residents there, with more people coming each year. Truth be told, Jacksonville's populace has been consistently expanding at a pace of about 2% every year, and their labor force is developing at a reliable rate too.

There are numerous explanations behind this development. First off, Jacksonville is likewise a major area in Florida that is home to four Fortune 500 organizations. The district additionally has an a-list medical care framework, with in excess of 20 emergency clinics and a developing bioscience network.

Market Statistics for Housing

- Average Sales Price - $189000
- Average Monthly Rent - $1409
- Average Household Income - $58709
- Population - 1.5 M
- One Year Job Growth Rate - 3.11 percent
- Seven Year Equity Growth Rate - 75 percent
- Eight Year Population Growth - 14.75 percent
- Rate of Unemployment - 3.0 percent

Quick Facts on the Housing Market

1. The area's populace has risen practically over 14% since 2000, which is higher than both Tampa's and Miami's.

2. Projection for job growth in Jacksonville is 39.21% throughout the following ten years.

3. In Jacksonville, the middle home cost is about $189,000, which is 15% below the nation's average.

4. A regular 3 room home can lease for around or more than the American average.

5. The development of the "Panama Canal" is assisting with carrying occupations into the Jacksonville territory ports. This is probably going to prompt much more growth in population.

6. The Jacksonville metro additionally offers a-list medical services, with in excess of 20 clinics and a developing bioscience network.

Employment Growth: Forbes additionally positioned Jacksonville #3 on their rundown of best urban areas in the country. The created jobs had a development pace of 3.11% this year. That is 111% quicker than the American average. The area additionally has a top-notch medical care framework.

Populace Growth: The populace in Jacksonville has grown practically 15% since 2000, and keeps on developing by a 2% every year. Future occupation development throughout the following ten years is projected at 39.21%.

Affordability: In Jacksonville, the middle home cost is $189,000, which is (15%) not exactly the country's average. An ordinary 3 room home can lease for more or about the same price as the nation's average.

4. Huntsville, Alabama

The fourth-biggest city in Alabama, Huntsville is only a 90-mile drive on I-65 traveling north from Birmingham. Established in 1811, Huntsville is known for its rich Southern legacy and a tradition of room missions. Huntsville really procured the moniker "The Rocket City" during the 1960s when the Saturn V rocket was created at Marshall Space Flight Center, which later made it feasible for Neil Armstrong and Buzz Aldrin to moonwalk.

Today, Huntsville is an acclaimed urban area in the Southeast aspect of the nation. Money magazine named Huntsville "one of the country's most affordable urban communities."

Huntsville is likewise notable for its innovation, space, and security businesses. The top military employer with more than 31,000 positions at Redstone Arsenal. The "NASA Marshall Space Flight Center" is the following biggest labor employer. Huntsville is additionally home to a few Fortune 500 organizations.

Huntsville is believed to be among the best places to purchase real estate rentals, as real estate market here offers extraordinary opportunities for today's investors. It's one of the country's most reasonable venture markets.

Market Statistics on Housing

- Average Home Price - $158750
- Average Month Rent - $1075
- Average Household Income - $49060
- Population - 462693
- One Year rate of Job Growth Rate - 2.76 percent
- Seven Year rate of Equity Growth - 34.53 percent
- Eight Year Population Growth - 10.35 percent
- Rate Unemployment - 2.3 percent

Quick Facts on the Housing Market

1. Huntsville is home to a few renowned Southern colleges, including Alabama A&M University, Oakwood University and the University of Alabama in Huntsville.

2. The U.S. Space and Rocket Center, Alabama's top paid vacation spot and the world's biggest space gallery, is likewise situated in Huntsville.

3. Huntsville is notable for its innovation, space, and businesses on defense.

4. This urban area is resident to a few Fortune 500 organizations, which give an expansive base of assembling, retail and administration enterprises to the region.

5. Huntsville keeps on driving the development in Alabama. In recent eight years the populace has developed over 10%, which is 80% quicker than the public national median.

6. Huntsville appreciates lower charge rates and high leases, which increases the return-on-investment.

Employment Growth: With the number of already present Fortune 500 companies present and the ones expected because of the city's booming economy, Huntsville labor employment is about to hit the roof.

Populace Growth: More individuals are moving to Huntsville more than most different urban communities over the United States. This kind of populace development, when combined with moderate land costs and employment development, is a positive marker that the Huntsville land market is solid.

Affordability: Huntsville does appreciates lower taxes and serious rents, in certain neighborhoods as high as 0.97% of the buy-to-lease ratio, which builds return on investment. What's more, the normal 3 room single-family home cost is around $158,750. That is 28% lower than the public normal.

5. Dallas, Texas

Situated in Northern Texas, Dallas is the fourth most crowded metropolitan region in the country. Truly, Dallas was one of the most significant communities for the oil and cotton businesses because of its key placement.

Over the past five years, numerous organizations from urban areas like Los Angeles and San Francisco have begun studying the country to locate the best urban areas for settlement, and a significant number of them have focused on Dallas as a prime location.

Market Statistics on Housing

- Average Median Home Price - $215000
- Average Monthly rent - $1624
- Average Household Income - $79893
- Population - 7.5 M
- One Year rate Job Growth - 2.70 percent
- Seven Year rate of Equity Growth - 80.67 percent
- Eight Year Population Growth - 17.33 percent
- Unemployment Rate - 3.1 percent

Quick Facts on the Housing Market

1. Dallas is marginally affordable compared to the normal homes across the country. In 2019, the middle price tag of 3 room family homes (single) in the Dallas metro zone sits at $215,000. This is 3.5% lower than the public median of $222,000.

2. Dallas provides investors with an occasion to build a passive month to month income. In 2019, the average monthly lease for 3 room homes in Dallas stood at $1,654. This is 0.77% of the price tag of $215,000. This is (0.75%) higher than the public median.

3. Dallas home estimations are rising quicker than other markets. Throughout the last 7 years (2012 to 2019), 3 room homes in Dallas have increased in value by 81%. During a similar period, 3 room home estimations increased in value by 55% across the country.

4. Dallas is the ninth most-crowded city in the U.S. what's more, it's a tremendous business and social center in Texas.

Employment Growth: This area enjoys a major job development. In the most recent year, Dallas added 100,200 new openings to their economy, with a yearly development pace of 2.70%. This is essentially higher than the normal average of 1.47%.

Populace Growth: Dallas' populace is developing quickly. In Dallas, the population has expanded by 17% in the course of the years, which is 201% quicker than the public average.

Affordability: In the neighborhoods where "RealWealth" individuals contribute, the middle cost of 3 room homes stands at $145,000 in 2019. This is 35% lower than the public median of $222,000.

6. Houston, Texas

When the then-President of the "Republic of Texas", Sam Houston, consolidated the "City of Houston" in 1837, the predominant business was railroad development. A great deal has changed from that point forward, however, the city's energy for methods of transportation has not.

What makes this city probably the best spot to purchase rentals? It has work development, populace development, AND it's still lovely darn moderate!

This city houses as much as 49 Fortune 1000 organizations, which is the second biggest centralization of some other city in the nation, behind just New York with 72.

Houston is a steady, landowner inviting business sector that offers both income and value development. Furthermore, you can still get properties well underneath their substitution esteem.

Market Statistics on Housing

- Average (present) Home Price - $175000
- Average monthly rent - $1517
- Average Household Income - $75377
- Population - 6.9 M
- One Year rate of Job Growth - 2.59 percent
- Seven Year rate of Equity Growth - 60.55 percent
- Eight Year Population Growth - 17.64 percent
- Rate of Unemployment - 3.5 percent

Quick Facts on the Housing Market

1. Houston is presently more moderate than most real estate markets in the country. In 2019, the average cost of three-room homes in Houston was $175,000. That's 21% lower than the national average of $222,000

2. Houston offers all investors a solid platform to create passive income monthly. In 2019, the average lease per month for 3 room apartments in Houston was $1,517. That's 0.87% of the price tag of $175,000 which is higher than the public cost-to-lease ratio (0.75%).

3. Houston home estimations have been rising more rapidly than the majority of the country's real estate markets. In 2012, 3 room apartments in Houston was $104,000 (on an average). Throughout the proceeding seven years, the value of the Houston apartments increased by 61%.

4. Houston was positioned by Forbes as the #10 best place for youthful entrepreneurs. Also, it was #2 best area to live on the planet (Business Insider).

Employment Growth: It's at present close to the top for work development in the country. Also, the typical cost for basic items is well underneath the nation's average.

Populace Growth: From 2010, Houston's populace has expanded by 18%. During that period, America's population developed by just 2.35%. The populace in Houston is growing 206% quicker than the average nationally. This reveals that individuals are moving to Houston massively than most other American urban communities.

Affordability: In 2019, the average cost of 3 room homes in Houston was $175,000. That's 21% lower than $222,000 (the national average). Houston additionally offers investors a solid platform to generate passive income per month.

7. Cleveland, Ohio

Cleveland (Ohio) remains a solid real estate market in the U.S, providing investors with high income and future development. With a labor force of more than 2 million individuals, The area is ranked the twelfth biggest economic region in the country. Situated on the south of Lake Erie, 60 miles west of the Pennsylvania outskirt.

Cleveland is still growing with as much as 15,000 people moving midtown, last summer. These re-settlers generally involved Millennials (from ages 18-34). Termed the "brain gain," the move was as a result of the 139% increase in the number of youthful occupants having degree certifications.

Why Downtown Cleveland? The region has encountered a renaissance in recent years, with an expected $19 billion (in development) since 2010. Just over the last three years, a green space of ten-acres in downtown was upgraded and has immediately a center for tourists and locals alike.

Market Statistics on Housing

- Average (present) Home Price - $138000
- Average Monthly Rent - $1143
- Average Household Income - $71582
- Population - 2.1 M
- One Year rate of Job Growth - 0.94 percent
- Seven Year rate of Equity Growth - 31.43 percent
- Eight Year Population Growth - 0.90 percent
- Rate of Unemployment - 4.2 percent

Quick Facts on the Housing Market

1. Fastest developing medical care economy. Resident to the incredibly famous Cleveland Clinic.

2. Nation's first Global Center for Health and Innovation.

3. Ten Fortune 500 organization base camp (Goodyear Tire, Cliffs, Natural Resources, Firstenergy, Sherwin Williams, Eaton Corporation, Travel Centers of America, Aleris, Parker Hannifin, Progressive Insurance, KeyCorp).

4. Home to three significant game groups that carry billions of dollars to the region consistently.

5. Job development proceeds to consistently grow at 0.94%.

6. In 2019, 3 room homes in Cleveland cost $138,000 (on an average). That's 38% less than the average.

Job Growth: The region's medical services and tech area is among the nation's fastest in growth. Recent college grads are moving into the territory quickly to make the most of the job openings. Companies like, The Cleveland Clinic, Eaton Corporation, and Key Corp.

Populace Growth: Although Cleveland's population has seen a decline in the last 8 years, the quantity of individuals moving to downtown Cleveland has risen (6,000 - 20,000 inhabitants). With new people (12,500) moving midtown last year, which comprised mostly of millennials, Cleveland is a goldmine.

Affordability: In the neighborhoods where "RealWealth" individuals are still investing, average value sits at $105,000 which is 53% lower than the general average.

8. Cincinnati, Ohio

Cincinnati is an historic and special city situated on the Ohio River. Winston Churchill once said that "Cincinnati is the most wonderful of the inland urban communities in the Union." It appears as though many individuals today concur with Mr. Churchill. This is one motivation behind why Cincinnati is probably the best if you want to invest in rentals.

With 2.2 million in population, the area is key to the 24th biggest U.S. metropolitan territory and it's still rapidly developing! Cincinnati and its neighbor, Dayton, are currently experiencing an upsurge in lodging, retail and business advancement across both Butler and Warren regions. As indicated by CNBC, an ongoing report positioned Cincinnati as one of 15 city's drawing in the most twenty to thirty year olds in 2018.

Cincinnati is a well-known destination for new and moving corporate companies, including 10 Fortune 500 organizations and 17 Fortune 1000 organizations.

These are all great signs for an investor looking for where to invest his or her resources. With a solid possibility of appreciation, Cincinnati should make any investor's top choice for investing in rental properties.

Market Statistics on Housing

- Metropolitan Population - 2.2 M
- Average Household Income - $80277

- Average (present) Home Price - $165000
- Average Monthly Rent - $1232
- One Year rate of Job Growth - 2.06 percent
- Seven Year rate of Equity Growth - 35.25 percent
- Eight Year Population Growth - 3.58 percent
- Rate of Unemployment - 3.8 percent

Quick Facts on the Housing Market

1. The region is among the country's 25 fastest growing areas with a consistently growing population.

2. A $350 million retail complex opened started in 2018.

3. Cincinnati and Dayton is the nation's fourth biggest inland center point.

4. Cincinnati is fourth in the US in new offices – including GE Aviation's new 420,000 square-foot (Class A) office grounds and another 80,000 sq ft Proton Therapy Center for research on cancer.

5. Cincinnati has additionally finished a $160 Million dollar ground expansion.

6. In 2019, the average rent per month for three-room homes was $1,232, which is 0.75% of the price tag of $165,000. This is directly in accordance with the public cost to-lease ratio of 0.75%.

7. Cincinnati was named, by Forbes, among the real estate's best markets in 2020.

Employment Growth: The Cincinnati metro region has the fourth biggest number of new companies in the country. Employment development in Cincinnati is growing at 40% quicker than the general average.

Population Growth: The area's population has grown to 3.58% recently. Despite the fact that this is underneath the national average, it's actually developing.

Affordability: In Cincinnati, you can still buy a completely revamped rental property in great neighborhoods for prices ranging from $123,000 to $150,000.

9. Chicago, Illinois

Known for its skyscrapers and Fortune 500 organizations, the Windy City is among a handful of American markets where you can still discover exciting opportunities to invest in.

The city's real estate prices are higher and also it has a "lower-than-average" employment. With these, Chicago may not appear to be an "acceptable" location to put resources into. However, remember, it is among the few urban areas in the country where lodging costs actually haven't transcended their 2006 levels. When searching for the best place with cash-flow and capital growth, you'll discover that certain areas offer homes at $128,000 to $210,000. These places have rent prices as high as 1.13% (above average) of the price tag each month!

The entirety of this is great news is for those looking for properties that are "under market value" that offer huge monthly income.

Market Statistics on Housing

- Metropolitan Population - 9.5 M
- Average Household Income - $84,000
- Average (present) Home Price - $210,000
- Average Monthly Rent - $1,679
- One Year rate of Job Growth - 0.80 percent
- Seven Year rate of Equity Growth - 41 percent
- Eight Year Population Growth - 0.29 percent
- Rate of Unemployment - 3.6 percent

Quick Facts on the Housing Market

1. Chicago is the third biggest city in the U.S and one of the best 5 most financially strong urban communities on the planet.
2. The average price of the normal 3 room home in Chicago metro zone was $210,000. That's 5% lower than the national average for 3 room homes.

3.   In the neighborhoods where RealWealth individuals invest, the average price tag in 2019 was $128,000. That's 42% unaffordability compared to the national average.

4.   The average lease in Chicago is over $1,679 every month, with more than half of the residents living on rent.

5.   83% of Chicagoans live for a year or two in one home.

6.   Chicago is home to 30 Fortune 500 organizations and flaunts a $500 billion GDP (Gross Domestic Product). That's more than that of both Belgium and Norway.

Job Growth: Chicago is the third biggest city in America and among the 5 strongest, economically urban areas on the planet. There are 30 Fortune 500 organizations settled in the region. In the previous year, Chicago added 37,900 new job openings to its economy.

Population Growth: The prices of real estate have increased inside Chicago's city limits. The result is that individuals are moving out of the city and into suburbia. Subsequently, prices in a portion of these areas keep appreciating. While the growth of the Chicagoan population is well beneath the national average, note that it's still growing well.

Affordability: Chicago is one of the last markets with its housing price still within its 2006 levels. This is due to the state's extreme laws on foreclosures. The average cost for a home in Chicago is $210,000, however, you can still discover homes in mid-level neighborhoods in the range of $128,000 and $210,000.

10. Indianapolis, Indiana

This is a region of over 2.1 million individuals. Indianapolis is the second biggest city in the Midwest and fourteenth biggest in the country. The city has emptied billions of dollars into rejuvenation and now positions among the best midtowns and most decent urban communities, as indicated by Forbes.

The price of housing and the yearly average cost for basic items in Indianapolis are well under the nation's average. Indy additionally has a solid, varying occupation market, extraordinary schools and colleges, and a lot of sports attractions. In 2019, the monthly average lease for three-room homes in Indianapolis was $1,172, which is 0.71% of the price tag of $164,400. This is marginally lower than the public cost to-lease proportion of 0.75%. What do these components imply regarding the potential of rental properties in Indianapolis? Expect to make big money once you get your homework done.

Market Statistics on Housing

- Metropolitan Population - 2.1M
- Average Household Income - $68,000
- Average (present) Home Price - $164,400
- Average monthly Rent - $1,172
- 1-Year rate of Job Growth - 0.81 percent
- Seven Year rate of Equity Growth - 45.00 percent
- Eight Year Population Growth - 8.25 percent
- Rate of Unemployment - 3.1 percent

Quick Facts on the Housing Market

1. 3 Fortune 500 Companies are headquartered in Indianapolis.

2. 7 new-age tech "Certified Technology Parks" having tax incentives to new businesses.

3. Big distribution centers including Fedex, Celadon Trucking, Amazon, Target.

4. Indy is the ONLY America metro territory to have "specialized employment concentrations" in every one of the 5 bioscience areas that were assessed: horticultural feedstock and chemical compounds; bioscience-related appropriation; medications and drugs, etc.

This is the reason it's made our rundown of the best places to purchase investment property

Employment Growth: Indianapolis remains among the fastest-growing centers for innovation, bioscience and Fortune 500 organizations in the country.

Population Growth: With a metropolitan territory of over 2.1 million individuals, Indianapolis is the second biggest city in the Midwest and fourteenth biggest in the U.S. Since 1989 Indy's populace has become over 36%, and keeps on developing at a pace of almost 1% every year.

Affordability: Indianapolis is among the few urban areas where you can buy like-new, rental prepared properties for $80,000 to $135,000. In 2019, the average monthly lease for three-room homes in Indianapolis was $1,172, which is 0.71% of the price tag of $164,400.

11. Detroit, Michigan

Wondering why Detroit is among the best cities for rentals? It's the biggest city in the territory of Michigan, also it is believed to be the car capital of the world. This is the reason numerous individuals know it by the moniker "Engine City." The metro region is home to General Motors, Ford Motor Company, Chrysler ("The Big 3" significant car organizations in Canada and United States).

Detroit is likewise home to Fortune 500 organizations (100), including Penske Automotive, Quicken Loans, Kellogg, Whirlpool, and Walmart.

Notwithstanding its longstanding epithet, a few of Detroit's quickest developing enterprises are in areas as differing as medical services, guard, aviation, IT and co-ordinations.

People like Dan Gilbert (the director and originator of Rock Ventures and Quicken Loans Inc, who also owns or has shares in several other companies) has moved various organizations to Detroit, putting over $1.6 Billion in the Detroit territory.

The many attractions in the city include Detroit Tigers, Detroit Lions, Detroit Red Wings, Wayne State University, University of Michigan, Beaumont Hospital, Fox Theater. Also, there's a bridge to Canada currently being constructed.

Lodging Market Statistics

- Metropolitan Population - 4.3M
- Average (present) Household Income - $75,000
- Average Monthly rent - $1,462
- One Year rate of Job Growth - 0.51 percent
- Seven Year rate of Equity Growth - 99.0 percent
- Eight Year Population Growth - 0.82 percent
- Unemployment Rate - 3.8 percent

Quick Facts on Housing

1. Detroit is house 100 Fortune 500 organizations, including Penske Automotive, Quicken Loans, Kellogg, and many more.

2. Despite its longstanding moniker, a few of Detroit's quickest developing enterprises are in areas as different as medical services, guard, aviation, IT and co-ordinations.

3. The Michigan Business Development Program gives awards, credits, and other monetary help to organizations.

4. Michigan has a level of 6% corporate personal expense, which is the least in the country.

5. Personal cash flow tax is also among the least in the country at 1.2%.

6. Michigan has a reduced cost for basic items than some other Midwestern state.

7. Since 2010, over 45,000 car producing companies have been added to the Detroit Metro, which is more than most other areas in the country.

Employment Growth: According to the U.S. Authority of Labor Statistics, the business rate in Detroit expanded by 0.82% from 2010 to July 2018. During that time-frame, the nation's occupation count expanded by 5.76%. Notwithstanding the area's slow/negative development, the Detroit metro actually beats the other market areas similar to it at pulling in the Millennials to their labor force.

Population Growth: People have been trailing organizations/occupations to "more affordable" urban areas. For instance, Billionaire Dan Gilbert (the executive and organizer of Rock Ventures and Quicken Loans Inc, among other companies) has moved various organizations to Detroit, with more than $1.6 Billion in assets invested in the area.

Affordability: In the Detroit neighborhoods where the RealWealth members have investments, the middle cost of 3 room homes in 2019 was just $87,000. This is 61% lower than the general average. This implies that Detroit is ripe for the taking as far as rental properties are concerned.

12. Atlanta, Georgia

Situated in the foothills of the Appalachian Mountains, Atlanta is the third-biggest metro district in the Southeast, behind the Greater Washington and South Florida zones.

For quite a long time, Atlanta experienced fast populace development to meet the rate of new job openings in the area, huge numbers of them in lucrative areas like manufacturing. Presently, Atlanta's development has eased back a little, yet there's still a lot of decent investment opportunities for smart investors. All you need is to know where to look and do your home-work.

Market Statistics on Housing

- Metropolitan Population - 5.9M
- Average Household Income - $77000
- Average (present) Home Price- $189900
- Average Monthly Rent - $1434
- One Year rate of Job Growth - 2.15 percent
- Seven Year rate of Equity Growth - 109.00 percent
- Eight Year Population Growth - 12.18 percent
- Rate of Unemployment - 2.9 percent

Quick Facts on the Housing Market

1. From 2018 to 2019, 3 room family homes (single) in the Atlanta metropolitan increased in value by 15.03%. This is higher than the general average of 9.90%. Over a 7-year time span, the housing market price appreciation peaked at 109%, which is 97% quicker than the average.

2. During that time-frame, rents for 3 room family homes (single) in Atlanta increased in value by 4.95%.

3. Over the previous 8 years, Atlanta's population saw a 12.18% development. That's 111% quicker than 5.76% (the national average).

4.   In recent years, 60,300 new job openings were in Atlanta (a yearly development pace of 1.96%). This is a higher rate than 1.73% (the national median).

Employment Growth: Recently, 53,700 new openings were made in Atlanta, which is a yearly development rate of 2.15%.

Population Growth: Over a 8 year span, Atlanta city grew in population by 12.18%. That is 111% quicker than the national median.

Affordability: In 2019, the middle price tag of 3 room single-family homes in Atlanta was $190,000. This is 15% lesser than the general median of $222,000 for 3 room houses. That great for prospective rental property investors.

13. Columbus, Ohio

The capital of Ohio, Columbus is the biggest city in the state. Lately, this city has risen as one of the country's most modern urban communities (in terms of technological sophistication). Columbus is home to the Batelle Memorial Institute, the world's biggest private innovative work establishment. The area also houses the Ohio State University, the country's third-biggest college grounds.

Columbus offers extraordinary opportunities for today's investors who are ready to seize the bull by the horn. This is particularly valid for the individuals who are searching for an area offering affordable investment, solid month to month income, and a decent chance for growth in value.

Market Statistics on Housing

- Average Sales Price - $183000
- Average Monthly Rent - $1310
- Average Household Income: $79694
- Population - 2.1 M
- One Year rate of Job Growth - 0.84 percent
- Seven Year rate of Equity Growth - 51.24 percent
- Eight Year Population Growth - 10.49 percent

- Rate of Unemployment - 3.7 percent

Quick Facts on the Housing Market

1. Columbus is very affordable. In 2019, most three-room homes in Columbus went for $183,000, which is 18% lesser than $222,000.

2. Sometimes single-family homes were valued for as much as 0.90% of the price tag. This is well over the general average in 2019.

3. Columbus is the fourteenth biggest city in the nation. Throughout the last eight years, Columbus' metropolitan population witnessed a growth of over 10%. That's faster than the average rate (5.76%).

4. The official Realtor website positioned Columbus as the fourth hottest market as regards housing in the nation.

5. Business Week named the area among the best urban areas to live and work in America.

Employment Growth: Columbus added more than 9,300 new job openings between 2018 and 2019. Though these statistics show a slower pace in terms of job growth, however, the development rate keeps on rising consistently.

Population Growth: The area has witnessed over 10% of population growth in the eight years. That is faster than the nation's average rate and also the area remains the fourteenth biggest city in the nation.

Affordability: You can still buy completely revamped properties in great neighborhoods for around $100,000 in Columbus if you know where to look.

14. Albuquerque, New Mexico

Situated in the Rio Grande Valley, Albuquerque is the most crowded city in the province of New Mexico and the 32nd-most crowded city in the U.S.

Renowned for its yearly Balloon Fiesta and as the setting for the record-breaking show "Breaking Bad," Albuquerque, New Mexico, is a socially rich and an excellent metropolitan territory. Albuquerque is at the focal point of New Mexico's "Technology Corridor,"

The area has a huge concentration of new-age tech companies and government establishments situated along the Rio Grande stream. It is additionally home to Intel, Sandia National Laboratories, Kirkland Air Force Base and four colleges. Furthermore, we can expect more positions and films emerging from the territory as Netflix plans to move its new American hub into the region.

Market Statistics on Housing

- Average Sales Price - $204000
- Average Monthly Rent - $1226
- Average Household Income - $65000
- Population - 915927
- One Year rate of Job Growth - 0.9 percent
- Seven Year rate of Equity Growth - 24 percent
- Eight Year Population Growth - 3 percent
- Rate of Unemployment - 4.5 percent

Quick Facts on the Housing Market

1. A typical three-room apartment in Albuquerque went for $204,000 in 2019. That's 8% lesser than the average nationwide value.

2. In 2019, the average price for the monthly lease of a three-room home was $1,670. That's 0.75% of the average price tag of $222,000.

3. Since 2010, the Albuquerque population has expanded by 2.96%. The nationwide population developed by 5.76% during that time frame. That implies that Albuquerque is witnessing stable population growth year after year.

4. From November 2018 to November 2019 jobs in the Albuquerque metropolitan expanded at a pace of 0.89%. This is slower when compared to the nationwide average.

Employment Growth: Between November 2018 and November 2019, the number of occupations in the Albuquerque metro expanded at a pace of 0.89, which is slower than the 1.47% development rate broadly during this period. Despite this fact, it's as yet a decent sign that more individuals will keep moving into the territory.

Population Growth: Since 2010, the populace in Albuquerque has expanded by 2.96%. Although this is not exactly the 5.76% development average, it shows that Albuquerque is witnessing a steady growth population annually. Note that this development isn't faltering, it's another pointer that Albuquerque's real estate market will keep on being steady in years to come.

Affordability: Houses in Albuquerque are valued to be 8% more affordable than the country's average.

15. Birmingham, Alabama

Situated in the lower regions of the Appalachian Mountains, Birmingham is a quite populous city in the province of Alabama and Jefferson County's county seat.

Atop the country's manufacturing age, the city's population growth was so amazing that they nicknamed it "Magic City." The moniker stuck when they found it was likewise the planet's only city where the three steel manufacturing materials (coal, limestone, and iron mineral) could be found normally within a 10-mile radius.

Still wondering why it's among the best places to invest in real estate? Indeed, over the previous decades, the city has gone through a significant renewal, turning into a publishing center, clinical research, construction, banking, and organizations offering various services.

Today, the Magic City is viewed as one of the country's most enjoyable urban areas on account of its energetic midtown, blossoming space network, and elite culinary scene. Also, Zagat voted the city #1 "Up-and-Coming Food City" in 2016.

Market Statistics on Housing

- Average Sales Price - $116000
- Average Monthly Rent - $1150
- Average Household Income - $67000
- Population - 1.2M

- One Year rate of Job Growth - 1.55 percent
- Seven Year rate of Equity Growth - 30.04 percent
- Eight Year Population Growth - 2.03 percent
- Rate of Unemployment - 2.5 percent

Quick Facts on the Housing Market

1. This is a very affordable area for investors with little capital. Housing costs are well below the nationwide average in the city, meaning that if you invest here, you'll be paying less than most other U.S. urban communities today.

2. Birmingham provides a platform for huge returns. 3-room single-family homes in the area can lease for over .99% of the price tag, which implies there's a solid income for you here.

3. Birmingham isn't one of those areas in the U.S that experience fluctuating prices that increases today and suddenly decrease tomorrow. This means investors can make a more steady income than numerous different U.S. urban communities. This also implies that it's safer to invest in this city than most markets in the country.

4. This is a consistently growing city because, throughout the previous 7 years, the city has witnessed both job and population development at a consistent yearly rate.

Employment Growth: From November 2018 to November 2019, Birmingham's city has expanded by a little under of 1.55% (6% higher than the nation's average). That means that Birmingham is generating more jobs for her citizens than most of today's U.S. urban communities.

Population Growth: Since 2010, the area's populace has developed by 2.03%. In spite of the fact that this is actually slower than the average, it shows a predictable development.

Affordability: Birmingham home estimations stand at 48% beneath the average.

16. Pittsburgh, Pennsylvania

Although Pittsburgh still seems to be a decent area to put resources into this city is not a top recommendation for prospective investors.

Having over 2.3 million in population, the Pittsburgh Metropolitan region is the 22nd biggest in the United States. The "Burgh" is known as "The City of Bridges" (for having a staggering 446 bridges), and "The Steel City" for its previous steel-producing base.

The area houses a few huge companies that enable the city keep its moderate and developing economy stable. This includes PNC (Pittsburgh National Corporation) Financial Services and Federated Investors. Its economy blossoms with technology, medical care, mechanical technology, glass, and financial organizations. The recent version of the film (The Dark Knight Rises) was recorded midtown.

The locale is additionally known for oil and petroleum production and is the central command to major international financial organizations.

Ranked among the 12 areas for investors to invest by the Pittsburgh Post-Gazette, the Burgh is likewise one of the top 10 markets in the country for growth.

Market Statistics on Housing

- Average Sales Price - $141000
- Average Monthly Rent - $1115
- Average Household Income - $59000
- Metropolitan Population - 2.3 M
- One Year rate of Job Growth - 0.68 percent
- Six Year rate of Equity Growth - 21.00 percent
- Five Year Population Growth - 1.00 percent
- Rate of Unemployment - 3.8 percent
- Rate of Unemployment - 3.8 percent

Quick Facts on the Housing Market

1. The selling price for 3 room family (single) apartments in Pittsburgh stays low at just $141,000 (average). Notwithstanding, in certain neighborhoods investors can buy homes for under $73,000.

2. Median monthly rent is $1,115 or 0.79% of the average price tag, which creates an opportunity for sizable and brisk returns on investments.

3. Pittsburgh is witnessing a consistent rise in the values of its houses with over 21% growth in the previous 6 years.

4. The area enjoys a stable employment growth in sectors like the medical sector, leisure and entertainment, and STEM (science, technology, engineering and mathematics) areas.

5. Pittsburgh houses up to 15 Fortune 500 organizations. The city is also home to the East Coast headquarter for Google and numerous other new-age tech businesses.

6. Business Times places the area at #1 among the top cities to move to and Zillow names it on its best 10 housing markets in the country.

Employment Growth: Although Pittsburgh has not been creating as many jobs as a number of U.S. urban communities, however, the metro region is currently on the rise in that area. For instance, 6,773 jobs were generated from the leisure & hospitality, health & education, business and professional administrations. The STEM sector also contributed its quota from September 2015 to 2016.

Nonetheless, 6,447 positions were lost from the merchandise-producing sectors. This almost caused the net decrease in the labor market for the metro territory.

Population Growth: Pittsburgh's general populace has experienced a decline since 2010, yet the millennial population has been developing. Indeed, in a recent report by Niche, Pittsburgh positioned #12 for best urban areas for persons aged 20 to 30.

This is great news for all prospective investors who may have their eyes on beginning their real estate journeys in the area. Also note that this is a city that naturally prefers renting apartments than purchasing (in 2017, college grads who were homeowners stood under 13%).

Affordability: Average cost of a 3 room single-family home in Pittsburgh was as low as $141,000 (on an average). This is 30% lesser than the nationwide average.

17. Kansas City, Missouri

Similar to Pittsburgh, Kansas does not hold a top spot on our recommended cities list for a prospective investor to practice rentals.

Generally known for its games, craftsmanship and culture, Kansas is among the list of the most moderate urban areas in the country to invest in. Since 2010, the populace in the metropolitan territory has expanded by 6.15%, adding up to 2.1 million individuals.

The city's gross territorial product increased by 2.9% in 2014. That is higher than the 2.2% national average. Kansas City has had its medical care, manufacturing, IT, and the vehicle industry flourishing. The city also had approximately 18,100 job openings from August 2017 to August 2018.

Positive news for all potential investors: as of late, numerous people have been following organizations/employment to "more affordable" urban areas, like Kansas City. The outcome is that these affordable business sectors are seeing a consistent increment in rental demand. This implies it's an awesome thing to be a landowner in Kansas City.

Market Statistics on Housing

- Metropolitan Population - 2.1M
- Average Household Income - $45000
- Average (present) Home Price - $162000
- Average Monthly Rent - $1275
- One Year rate of Job Growth - 1.67 percent
- Six Year rate of Equity Growth - 17.00 percent
- Seven Year Population Growth - 5.72 percent
- Rate of Unemployment - 3.9 percent

Quick Facts on the Housing Market

1. Kansas City has gotten perhaps the hottest location for tenants, which thusly has increased the demand for more accessible homes and lofts for lease.

2. There are countless moderate homes available in the city including bank-owned and pre-disclosure properties. These properties are estimated to be around $100,000 to $120,000. The price on an average in this city is $162,000.

3. Average lease, monthly begins from $1,275 per month. The single-family income is about $45,000 in Kansas.

4. Employment kept on expanding by 1.67% in 2018, which includes about 18,100 jobs.

Employment Growth: Kansas City has become a significant area for manufacturers, medical services, IT as well as the auto sector. This includes about 18,100 jobs, a year ago.

Population Growth: as of late, numerous Americans have been following organizations/occupations to "more affordable" urban communities, including Kansas City. This means more people will be seeking to rent in the city.

Affordability: The average cost for apartments in Kansas City is $162,000. Be that as it may, the metro region has an enormous number of moderate homes available, including bank-owned and pre-disclosure properties with values ranging from $100,000 to $120,000. $1,275 is the average cost of rent on a monthly basis.

18. St. Louis, Missouri

Although St. Louis is not highly recommended for potential investors, it still makes our list and below is the reason why.

Home to over 2.8 million individuals, this metropolitan region is the 21st biggest metropolitan in the nation. It's additionally one of the most steady and affordable markets for any real estate investor who knows his/her onions. Today in St. Louis an investor can buy single-family home for a meager $120,000 and lease it for a little under 1% of the price tag.

St. Louis is mainstream among investors dealing in real estate, why? This is due to its steady economy, developing tech hub, huge metro populace, and most particularly, the affordability of its housing market.

Although the average home cost is still beneath $200,000, there are numerous pockets of the metro zone with much more affordable houses ($120K-$130K). These have an average month to month rent price of $1,100-$1,200.

Tenants make up 32% of the market in this city and this figure is projected to increase as the educated millennials keep on relocating to the area. This projection is based on the city's housing affordability.

Market Statistics on Housing

- Average Sales Price from 2018 to 2019 - $176000
- Average Monthly rent (2018-19) - $1269
- Average Household Income (2018-19) - $60000
- Population from 2018 to 2019 - 2.8 M
- One Year Job Growth Rate (2018-19) - 0.72 percent
- Five Year rate of Equity Growth (2018-19) - 27 percent
- Six Year Population Growth (2018-19) - 0.63 percent
- Rate of Unemployment (2018-19) - 4.50 percent

Quick Facts on the Housing Market

1. St. Louis prices are reasonable. On an average, a normal three-room apartment goes for $176,000 in St. Louis. That's 12% lower than the general average.

2. Monthly lease, (on an average) for a normal three-room home is $1,269 in St. Louis. This figure sits at 0.72% of the average price ($176,000).

3. From July 2010 to July 2017, the St. Louis metropolitan statistical area (MSA) witnessed a population growth of 0.63%. In spite of the fact that this development is essentially less than 5.29% (the national average) yet the populace is still developing.

4. From June 2017 to 2018, the metro area added 9,900 new job openings (an annual growth of 0.72%). During that same time-frame, over 2.4M jobs were generated across the nation.

Employment Growth: With an added 9,900 new jobs around 2017 and 2018 St. Louis is steadily growing its labor force. Although the job creation rate is slow in the city, however, you should note that positions have been made AND individuals have been moving to the area. All in all, slow growth is still growth regardless.

Population Growth: Since 2010, the city's populace rose by 0.63%. That figure might not mean much but projections for the future are very promising.

Affordability: In St. Louis investors can buy completely remodeled properties in great neighborhoods for under $127,000. Now that's a whopping 37% lower rate than the nation's average.

Conclusion

Rental properties is a decent investment for all prospective investors who may or may not have a decent capital to begin their real estate investment journey. However, once you have the necessary tools and do your home-work, the sky is your limit.

Chapter 8 – Strategic and Tactical Suggestions to Reduce the Cost of Managing Your Real Estate

You know the familiar axiom that goes, "you need cash to bring in cash and "you have to spend money to make money"? All things considered, this platitude is valid. Notwithstanding, with regards to real estate investing, there just might be a couple of stunts that you can pull to limit your monthly costs. For example, eliminating renovation costs or leasing of rental properties to the right occupants.

There are numerous strategies any real estate investor can practice to diminish costs and save-up the additional cash for other purposes.

To a real estate investor, the primary inquiry that springs up in their minds while anticipating their income is "Which is wiser, increasing income or cutting-down on expenses? Cash flow has a straightforward equation:

Saving = Income – Expenses.

Saving is more important since it shows up first in that equation. To save more, investors in real estate can either decrease expenses, increase income or do both simultaneously.

1. Decreasing expenses

If your primary focus is on reducing your costs, it is tied in with economizing. If you don't have any idea on how to build your income, decreasing expenses is the most effortless course to expand your total assets.

Firstly, exploit the real estate tax break to the fullest! The investors have an immense bit of leeway with regards to taxes. With the correct mindset, you can profit enormously from this chance.

- Deductions: A real estate investor has the capacity to deduct costs related with their investments. For example, Mortgage, loan interest and office costs.
- Capital Gains: Through capital profits, investors can deduct what they owe in taxes from the gains earned in business.

- Depreciation: A real estate investor may choose to deduct his or her losses if the investment property's value drops.

2. Seek modest labor

Just like any other venture, the difficult time and money consuming part of the business is labor. Labor is costly. Could an investor actually reduce the cost of labor when investing in real estate? All things considered, other than you doing the job yourself, there are other ways to do this too.

For example, you could employ an intern. The cool thing about interns is that they can work for free or close to it. Interns in real estate can do a significant part of the work, so you won't need to do it all by yourself.

3. A property well-kept is a keeper

Ensuring you maintain your rental property can assist you with saving a ton of your initial capital, for a long time. As an investor, you can decrease your repetitive costs by supplanting the high-end items with effective and moderate ones.

For instance, supplant an old window that may disintegrate earlier with a reasonable one that isn't so costly. Mortgage holders generally shy-away from fixing or refreshing their home in dread of these exuberant costs. However, these days everything is accessible in a wide scope of costs.

4. Partnering in Real Estate

Obviously, this is probably the most ideal way to limit your real estate expenses. Get a partner for yourself that has enough capital. Trust is also very important in this real estate venture. If you are reluctant to work with somebody, then look for a person from whom you can obtain the required capital. Furthermore, recollect that you have up to 1,000,000 different kinds of credits available to you, so don't be frightened to request help.

All in all, the real estate business isn't all about having various investment properties but, having the capacity to manage your property successfully. How about we take a step back and examine the various ways available, for you to make the most profit from your rentals venture.

- Reduce vacancy: One superb way to limit vacancies is to seek out a long-term inhabitant, so you don't need to manage high turnover. Each time there's an opening will cost you 8.3% of your possible yearly income. That is a ton of cash lost in one year. Therefore concentrate on keeping your property constantly occupied.

- Minimize turnover: This is a devourer as far as rental properties is concerned. There are promoting costs, the expense of painting and fixing walls as well as supplanting flooring that your past occupant would have lived with. One of your objectives ought to be to discover quality occupants that will keep your rental property in good shape and pay lease reliably.

  When you locate these inhabitants, do what you can to keep them! You consistently need to search for such occupants that are faithful, so pick shrewdly and cautiously.

- Stand firm against late payments: Showing regard and kindness to a tenant should not include being a weakling when it comes to leasing payments. Collections are not among the most agreeable duties of being a proprietor, however, it is vital to running your business profitably. Ensure your inhabitants comprehend that this is a business, they signed an agreement, and it is your duty to finish the transaction.

So know this, that being in real estate doesn't automatically mean you need to overspend all the time. Investors can expand their profits and reduce stress by exploiting the tips discussed here. What's more, remember that if there is a will, there is a way, and there is definitely always a strategy for lessening your monthly costs.

Ways Investors and Property Managers are Controlling Costs

Most investors and property managers are rearranging their work and how they oversee units and occupants. If you presently deal through a property management organization, by now you probably already have a new point of view on how to reorient your business.

Savvy property management is generally about technique because once costs begin to move, it's practically difficult to prevent the circumstance from playing out completely to a disastrous end.

Tenant and maintenance management remains the most difficult components of the business for landlords & property managers. Old-school property management style usually employs a reactive approach to the issue. This is the typical methodology of most landowners since they're left with an outdated framework. It's the main source of the daily stress that the landlords go through.

New-age property managers adopt internet property management software to establish a totally new relationship with their occupants. Undoubtedly, automating property management tasks with technology is a real life-saver. It's an entirely different way of thinking and it's in line with present-day occupants.

10 Ways to Manage Costs Forever

1. Select your investments carefully – old, frail structures or units mean something bad if you don't have a dependable contractor or landowner to deal with the steady fixes and the proper maintenance plans.

2. Spend on high-quality water heaters – an awful thermostat or thermocouple is a disaster ready to happen when the heaters develop a fault. Check the tank-less heaters and the gas fired. Those make for happy tenants (lucky as well) and save energy. Also if breakdowns happen they're simpler to fix.

3. Purchase high caliber A/C units – they last way longer, which implies less exorbitant fixes and time spent. Shop for dependable hardware.

4. Seek the services of a property manager (in case you're a housing (multifamily) investor – the expense of a property management organization is not encouraging but having to manage high volume properties and inhabitants will prove to be very problematic.

5. Take your time when selecting your occupants – Low-cost tenants are the best. You probably won't have issues finding or keeping inhabitants in these times, however, they can harm your property and cost you a ton of time. Take your time to screen tenants.

6. Stay atop of all expenses, contractors, fixes – Major misfortunes happen between the lines in a manner of speaking (unnecessary fixes, overcharging and bad repair services)

7.	Use property management software to automate the maintenance of your property – Using paper tickler documents and spreadsheets to manage things will prove to be a total time waster.

8.	Simplify your bookkeeping – Employ the use of property management software to record your costs and to save your mind from stress.

9.	Make sure your landlord teaches your tenants on the operation of tools – This is important to avoid unnecessary destruction of property. Discuss the rent agreement and educate them on how to take care of the yard, carport, wood flooring and how illicit pets can harm deck and covering. Discussions on these issues will assist your tenants to become more aware of the property and how to properly manage it.

10.	Keep tenants connected with the management software's communication power – This tool helps with rent payment, tenant relations and many more. At last, this prompts reduced tenant turnover, quiet and focused inhabitants, and generally a decrease in issues for you to tackle.

Chapter 9 – How to Buy Cheap Foreclosure

Before the advent of the '08 & '09 mortgage crisis, purchasing a foreclosed house was a troublesome enterprise. The bargain-hunters in real estate had to filter through reams of filings or follow the courthouse auctions. The "subprime meltdown" induced rush of foreclosures did not only expanded the number of accessible properties; it additionally made it simpler to discover and procure them.

Presently the search for foreclosures is quite similar to the search for any other kind of property. Foreclosed properties are accessible in all real estate markets the nation over. This gives rise to both investors and homeowners.

Ways for Investors to Discover Foreclosed Homes

One can discover foreclosed homes through the MLS (multiple listing service) sites and periodicals through internet searches, local newspapers, and so on. In local MLS postings, foreclosed properties may not get featured; the properties may be disclosed in the property's description.

A better route is through the numerous sites that are focused on foreclosed homes and properties. For example, Fannie Mae's HomePath website. Another way is through certain financial companies, like the "Bank of America" that dedicate pages to helping investors discover foreclosed properties.

Moneylenders, through the realtors, are progressively selling assets that were seized; therefore, always ask the real estate agent or broker about them. Certain real estate gurus specialize in foreclosed homes.

Reason Foreclosed Homes are More Affordable

The greatest advantage of a foreclosed home is, obviously, their "marked-down cost." These homes are usually lower than other comparable properties in a similar region (termed "comps" "comparables" in broker terms). Foreclosed properties come with major discounts below the market price. The buyers may likewise exploit the extra savings with advantages, like, decreased initial installments, lower interest rates, or the removal of appraisal charges and some closing costs.

What makes this such a stand-out deal? If the home is in the short-sale or pre-foreclosure stage, the owners have stuck a money related predicament—and their time is running out. They need to empty the property and get whatever they can while they still can, else they lose it. So, these dealers aren't haggling from a place of solidarity. While it might appear to be brutal to exploit others' mishaps, purchasers can profit here.

They can profit more if the property has been seized. The sheriff's office isn't keen on clinging to a house, and banks would prefer not to be in the landowner business. The financial institutions normally prefer to free themselves of this kind of property quickly (at a sensible cost, obviously). Once again, purchasers will naturally exploit this circumstance.

Lastly, foreclosed properties are generally sold "with no guarantees" (if there's harm, the proprietor's fixes aren't part of the issue). As those who purchase used-cars and vintage-furniture enthusiasts know, "with no guarantees" converts into a discount obviously, since it can be a two-edged blade.

Is it Advisable to Purchase a Foreclosed Home?

For the savvy purchaser who knows how it all works, a foreclosed home can be the best deals ever.

You can probably buy an abandoned house at a significant discount, renovate it, live in it, or sell it for a pure profit.

As it may, new studies reveal that's getting harder to discover foreclosure deals. There aren't as available as there used to be.

Anyway, is it justified to go through the trouble of discovering and buying a dispossessed home?

That all relies upon where you discover one and the deals you can get off of it.

Where to Discover Foreclosed Homes Today

A new report by ATTOM Data Solutions turned up some fascinating discoveries regarding foreclosures.

The research revealed that over 1.5 million American homes were empty in the final quarter of 2019. Yet, just 288,000 homes were going through the foreclosure procedures.

Furthermore, the percentage of "zombie foreclosures" (which are relinquished homes) has fallen to 2.96% of every foreclosed home. That's down from 2016's 4.7% and another 3.2% in 2019's third quarter.

ATTOM's research likewise found that the zombie foreclosure rates are higher in the following cities:

- 10.5% in Washington, D.C.
- 7.9% in Kansas
- 7.9% in Oregon
- 7.4% in Montana
- 6.7% in Maine
- 5.8% in New Mexico

The states in the U.S. where actual zombie properties are high are:

- 2266 properties in New York
- 1461 properties in Florida
- 892 properties in Illinois
- 823 properties in Ohio
- 398 properties in New Jersey

What's more, among postal divisions with a populace of 10,000 (minimum) and a minimum of 1,000 empty properties, the majority of zombie properties were recorded in:

- 31.2% vacancy rate in Flint, Michigan
- 28.3% vacancy rate in the Greater Chicago area
- 25.9% vacancy rate in Hilton Head, South Carolina
- 18.6% vacancy rate in Cleveland, Ohio
- 17.6% vacancy rate in Indianapolis, Indiana
- 17.3% vacancy rate in St. Louis, Missouri

So in case you're searching for a foreclosed property deal, these are the best places to begin your search.

Purchasing Foreclosed Homes: The Pros and Cons

Foreclosure homes are tempting because they frequently come at nice bargains.

That is particularly obvious when home costs keep on expanding each year. Be that as it may, purchasing a foreclosure property additionally comprises some dangers as well.

For instance, numerous foreclosed homes are bought at live sell-offs held at the courthouse in a neighborhood. Purchasers generally can't enter these properties to do an investigation. Also, they might be needed to pay money at the auction instead of taking a home loan credit.

Likewise, foreclosures are typically rarely well-managed properties. So it's simple for a purchaser to disparage the cost expected to do the important fix work.

There may also be outstanding liens that the purchaser may accidentally get answerable for, such as taxes, homeowner association (HOA) dues, mechanics liens, and many more.

Ways to Discover Foreclosed Homes

The primary test is locating the foreclosures close to you. To help your pursuit, attempt these:

• Employ a real estate agent's services of a realtor who is knowledgeable as regards buying foreclosures.

•	Check within your county. Contacting your county clerk's office could be very decisive here. Also, some may naturally post foreclosed homes on a weekly basis on their official websites.

• Scour official bank webpages. Banks usually post their for-sale foreclosed properties on the web.

- Search the "homes for sale" listings on the United States Department of Housing & Urban Development website.

- Search through online auction portals such as Hubzu, Xome, and Auction.

Except you've previously purchased foreclosed properties, you should talk with an expert before doing any deals on your own. It tends to be a very confounding ordeal to experience.

This is particularly the case for "zombie properties," which will probably still come with files containing the former proprietor's name.

How to Purchase Foreclosures

With regards to paying for foreclosed properties, your alternatives are genuinely restricted.

Strategies for financing the purchase of a foreclosed property:

- With the assistance of a home loan broker
- Using cash at an auction or bank
- With a hard-money credit
- With the federal housing authority (FHA) 203k fix loan
- With Freddie Mac's "CHOICERenovation" credit
- Other possible mortgage alternatives

Most foreclosed houses are bought using cash. Also, one probably has to work with a home loan broker. The broker probably has different credit options accessible from numerous moneylenders.

Among such brokers may be private moneylenders who give "hard cash" advances.

Today, it's much easier to access hard money loans at more sensible rates than in previous years.

Investors may purchase a foreclosed home "as-is" using hard money credits. Then fix it up and renegotiate with a standard mortgage agency at a lesser loan fee.

However, you're wondering if you can purchase a foreclosed home with a federal housing authority advance? Yes, this is achievable via a "federal housing authority" 203k credit. With that loan, you finance the buy and renovate the foreclosed house.

Check out programs such as "CHOICERenovation" from Freddie Mac or the FHA 203k. These credits permit you to carry out fixed costs using the loan.

Implication of Fewer Foreclosures on the Housing Market

Todd Teta who's "ATTOM Data solutions" chief producer, clarified what having lesser foreclosures would mean for the industry.

He said, "One of the most noticeable indications of the housing market crash during the Great Recession continues to recede within the past."

Bits of zombie foreclosures continue. Yet, many states in America face less and less of the void, rotting properties that were emblematic of the aftermath of the crash during the downturn.

Lots of foreclosure deals have dragged on for a long. This scenario has continued for a long. Now the borrower has decided to leave the property before selling at some auction. Sometimes the seller might even choose to repossess the property.

Reasons It's Getting Harder to Discover Foreclosures

It's harder to discover decent foreclosure deals these days basically because there aren't a lot of foreclosed homes in the market anymore. That is particularly evident in business sectors where homebuyers' request is more prominent than homes available to be purchased.

Experts believe that around 4% of home loans are in some phase of delinquency in a typical market, while another 1% is in foreclosure.

When the foreclosure crisis is at its peak, about 12% of home loans were reprobate, and foreclosures recorded 4%. So there was a record number of troubled properties flooding the market. However, today, marginally more than one-portion of 1% of home loans are in foreclosures.

The main explanation behind this is that, over the years, moneylenders have made it harder to get loans. In recent times it's very hard for anyone except the most qualified borrowers to access home loans.

In addition, home prices have continued to sky-rocket. This has led directly to record levels of mortgage holder value.

Experts believe that having more equity empowers distressed property holders. It enables them to carry-out deals to avoid losing their home to foreclosures.

Find a Deal on Foreclosed Homes

The result of the present low rates of mortgage is that homes will become more affordable. Thusly, there will be fewer homes going into foreclosure. However, there's a flip side. If you can discover and finance foreclosed properties, you could get an amazing deal in the present low-rate market.

The idea is to have a low rate deal at hand so that you can lock into it once you discover the property you're searching for.

Chapter 10 – Look at MLS Reports to Discover How Long a Property Has Been Listed

An MLS (Multiple Listing Service) is an information base comprising broker-listed homes. The only people who can access this service are the realtors and other affiliate gurus.

What's a multiple listing service?

This is a private, web-based database utilized by realtors to facilitate the purchasing and selling of homes. Each for-sale home listed by a realtor gets recorded in an MLS except if it's particularly excluded. Just realtors and other expert subsidiaries can get to the MLS. However, that doesn't mean a home buyer or seller can't get comparable data somewhere else.

Other well-known websites, like Trulia and Zillow, may also contain a significant number of similar postings. However, these two may not give-out the kind of comprehensive data that MLS is known for.

How the MLS Works

They are regional, with over 800 across the nation. The "Listing brokers" enter the information about a house that is available to be purchased. They also offer to split the commission with any dealer who helps bring a buyer.

Listings comprise the complete particulars about a home, including the location, age, area, number of rooms, number of showers, redesigns, and school locale. It incorporates other key details, like, a seller's favored sort of financing and photos of the property.

Most times, homebuyers mistakenly believe they can get to this data. However, the general public's information is normally restricted and can be obsolete or even inaccurate.

Ways to get the MLS Listings

As stated earlier, although numerous sites can provide homebuyers with a rundown of available homes, not many give the extensive information found in an MLS. However, your realtor can furnish you with information from an MLS.

There are numerous kinds of reports a purchaser can get, so approach your agent for the most detailed MLS report available. An agent can will type-in your name, email, and home preferences into the MLS search portal, so it will automatically send you messages of the latest listings.

Be aware that every agent cannot set up a quest for you other than the active listings. It is for you to indicate any extra data you might require. For example, value reductions, forthcoming deals, or sold deals information will not be automatically given to you.

Additionally, you can widen your search within these parameters to accommodate more criteria, like price ranges (from low to high), the number of rooms and showers, carports, pools and spas, area, etc.

It would help if you endeavored to define your prerequisites as plainly as possible, contingent upon your needs. Notwithstanding, if you get too specific with your search, you could pass up on several opportunities. It's ideal for keeping it, to some degree, general since certain MLS information fields probably won't contain data because of human errors.

Normally, purchasers need to know how long a house has been available. DOM (Days on Market) alludes to the number of days for which a listed property has been active on the MLS before it becomes "pending." Pending is when a seller has accepted an offer, but all transactions have not been done yet.

Numerous variables impact the days a property stays available. Factors like the economy, rivalry, and the "showing criteria" are some of the very important factors that can determine the DOM of a home. Numerous realtors utilize a strategy termed "relisting" to make homes that have been long on the listing look more appealing to purchasers.

Average Days on Market

Numerous agents will allude to DOM as "average days on the market." This figure is calculated by adding all the days a listing has been used on the market. Then divide the outcome by the quantity of all the listings. In a fast-moving business sector, the DOM is commonly higher since it takes more time to sell. However, in a seller's market, the DOM is typically less.

The real estate agents determine the average DOM by calculating the last 1-6 months of sold listings. For example, if six listings were entered as "pending" on December second. Three of those listings were available for five days, one was available for 21 days, and two were recorded for 30 days before accepted offers.

If you add up all the days on every listing market, you'll get 96 days. Divide that number by 6 listings to calculate the average DOM for a property that has been listed for 16 days.

DOM Matters to Sellers

Which is more significant? The 16 average DOM or the number of days a property has been made available on the MLS?

As a seller in a market with 16 days (average DOM) and your home has been available for 17 days, your property has fallen into the lower 50% of homes sold over the earlier month. Analysis has revealed that the more days a property stays on as available, the lesser the seller's chances of getting their asking price.

The perspective of the Buyers on DOM

Once a purchaser sees a property with extended days, as a rule, they reach one of the conclusions below:

- The seller is getting desperate and may sell for a lesser offer.

- The dealer is requesting more than the actual worth of the house.

- There's probably some problem with the property. Maybe a deformity that made different purchasers leave it.

Although those conclusions are quite valid, a home might remain on the listing for multiple reasons other than requiring exorbitant fixes or the "work to meet standards":

- Overpricing: This is the most widely recognized reason for houses that spend many days on the market. In a bid to get the listing, some agents may have deceived the seller into pricing the home beyond what the market can afford.

- The market effect: Many sellers could fix their minds on a price while prepared to stand by it until the market gets up to speed to their optimal value point. This commonly happens when the market is set up to favor purchasers.

- When the home is either unsuitable or inaccessible for inspection: If at that moment, the property is housing tenants, it very well may be hard to reach an agreement with the inhabitants. In some cases, dealers will list a property before they're prepared to let purchasers see them.

- Restrictive showing times: Certain sellers believe a purchaser will submit to strict showing times, convenient for sellers. Purchasers will, in general, visit homes according to their timetables. If your house isn't accessible for inspection when the purchaser wants to see it, they'll likely not see it.

- Agent issues: Buying agents are expected to reveal all listings for which a buyer shows interest, yet numerous agents abstain from showing homes that don't pay as high a commission as other contending properties.

- If the home has only one photo in the MLS: purchasers will probably disregard the posting will limit images and look rather at homes that have different images.

Relisting to Reset the DOM

One common practice among realtors is to withdraw a posting from MLS for a while; then, at a later date, they relist it as a new home. Specialists relist to show zero days since purchasers are more inclined toward new listings.

Numerous purchasers dislike this practice since it's deceptive. This strategy means that the DOM on a property is probably not accurate. Thus if purchasers become mindful of it, it might unfavorably influence the offer of the home.

It's not strange for a home to sell inside five days in the wake of returning as a new listing after it was already available for 60 to 90 days.

At times listings may expire. Many agents take a posting for 90 days, then another one snaps up the listing once the clock goes down.

Ways to Determine the Cumulative DOM

A few MLS systems do not allow agents to pull back a listing and relist without expiring or canceling the house first. In either case, it's generally simple for an accomplished agent to decide the number of days available. However, it's not as simple for a purchaser.

One method for learning the total number of days a property has spent on the market is to enter the property's location into MLS to locate a copy, terminated, or a withdrawn listing. A few systems on MLS have changed how postings are accounted for and will remember to share the cumulative days on a listing market.

The web can likewise give you answers. You can enter the property address into a certain search engine. This usually comes up with its past online listings as well as the new one.

In case you're partnering with a local specialist, they ought to be able to make a smart guess on an hour-long, the property has been available, recorded, and by whom.

There may have been a decrease in value, so the specialist will feel justified in sharing such information with you. Inquire as to whether the listing has been terminated, dropped, withdrawn, or even relisted.

If your home's history has sparked up curiosity within you, you should know that fundamental insights regarding it are available on Zillow or Redfin websites. Indeed, even your home's title report, which you or your agent should pull retained, contains helpful data.

However, if you need to dig further, there are a few devices that can assist you with investigating your home's proprietors, fascinating events that may have occurred in or close to your property. One could even see a picture of what it looks like. Thus keep digging.

Property Listings

The following is a list of websites that will give you vital details about a property you're thinking about purchasing:

Trulia's property sitemap

This is one proper place to begin your search. The site has more information to give than a standard Trulia search. If that's not enough, contact the real estate agent who helped you purchase the house. He can get the data on the MLS listings. The rundown of approaches to find the historical backdrop of a home is unlimited. You can search out an address and discover a lot, including pictures, maps (with boundaries), zoning, and the owner of multiple properties.

DiedInHouse

Yes, this one may seem a little morbid, but it can be decisive. DiedInHouse is a website that will let you know (you guessed right) if someone has kicked the bucket in your home. There are occasions in which realtors will need this data. However, numerous states don't need it. Therefore if you don't ask, you probably won't know.

For $12, the site will aggregate a report that reveals to you if and when a demise happened. It will also inform whether any meth activities or fire accidents ever took place in your house.

Historical Maps of Your City

Some urban areas have historical maps that enable you to search by address. It has not been affirmed if they also show pictures. However, you can check it out. Investors can look up photographs of places of interest; for example, the website "WhatWasThere" is a good start. The following are a couple of maps for some major cities in America:

- New York City
- Philadelphia
- San Francisco
- Los Angeles

Investors may also check out their home's "Google Street View" so long as they do not expect to find some ancient history. Enter your address on Google Maps, click on your home's photograph to get to Street View, and then search for the timeline.

Public Records

To locate your home's past proprietors or the buy history, you'll need to visit your county's tax assessor's office or county recorder. It all relies upon the kind of search and the data you are seeking. You can find property deeds, past proprietors, lawsuits, any encumbrances on the house, and so forth.

You can even observe the individual history, for example, if a proprietor is separated or bankrupt. Yes, it might seem unbelievable but, that sort of thing is an openly available report.

The local library in your area may likewise be able to help you in your search. Even your city's "Department of Building and Safety" may permit you to look into the names of those who worked on constructing the house.

Neighbors

On a less technical note, learning things regarding your home's history may be as straightforward as checking with your neighbors. Duh! If they've been in the region for some time, they probably have certain information that you may never discover in any openly available reports. You'll be surprised by the things you can learn from the individuals in your locale.

Chapter 11 – Purchase Money: Mortgage/Seller Financing

Purchase money loans are credits given to the purchaser of a home by the seller. It is likewise referred to as owner/seller financing.

A Purchase Money Loan

Once a potential homebuyer cannot meet all the requirements for a conventional mortgage loan from a bank, they can get an advance from the seller. This is what real estate investors and realtors' term purchase money loan.

These loans are frequently utilized by purchasers who do not fit the bill for a traditional loan due to a poor credit score. Individuals who need more money for the initial payments also seek this sort of financing.

If you are offered seller financing, you still should endeavor to carry out an independent appraisal to guarantee that you are not overpaying or taking a bigger loan than the property's worth.

The expression "purchase money loan" sometimes refers to any home loan used to purchase a home or property. This is to separate credits used for buying a property apart from refinanced mortgages or home equity loans.

Other similar terms are purchase-money mortgage, owner's loan, owner financing, seller's loan, and seller financing.

How This Loan Works

Purchase money loans normally take either one of the following forms.

- If the seller has no mortgage, the purchaser pays an initial installment, and the rest of the house's expense is financed through a purchase money loan from that seller. The seller then sets up the interest rate and monthly payment.

- In a situation where the seller has a mortgage on the home, the purchaser agrees to pay up the seller's mortgage payments. The seller's purchase money loan is what's left after you subtract the up-front payment from the rest of the mortgage amount. The purchaser pays the loan in bits equivalent to the home loan's monthly cost until the home is there's.

- The purchaser buys the home with an initial payment and a traditional bank loan. However, he or she doesn't fit the bill for a loan that's big enough to cover the cost of the house. The bit of the price tag not covered by the loan or the bank credit is the purchase money loan.

If an investor uses a traditional loan, they should inform the moneylender regarding any additional financing obtained. As well as any seller financing acquired.

A seller who provides loans must consent to state laws concerning licensing, the home loan's length, and usury laws. Notwithstanding,

Purchase money loans regularly come with higher interest rates than conventional ones due to the borrower's poor credit.

Hard Money Loan versus Purchase Money Loan

Purchase Money Loan

- Is financed via the seller
- Terms concerned with the seller's current home loan or the borrower's credit record

- Authorization is usually slow.
- They are frequently used by borrowers who struggle to pass for a conventional mortgage loan.

Hard Money Loan

- Financed through a conventional moneylender
- Terms are dependent on the borrower's collateral.
- Endorsement typically faster
- They are frequently used by borrowers who struggle to pass for a conventional mortgage loan.

Regardless of the definition applied, purchase money loans are dependent on the borrower's reliability. The dealer or other bank faces a challenge that the borrower probably won't reimburse the credit. If that occurs, the property enters foreclosures and becomes a property of the moneylender.

Borrowers regularly utilize the hard cash loan, like the purchase money loan, with helpless credit records. however, it is done through a bank or other customary moneylender and includes utilizing the property as security. The financing depends on the value of the property and not the borrower's reliability.

Kinds of Purchase Money Loans

The regular purchase money loan is from the seller to the purchaser. They employ comparative terms similar to the credit you get from a bank or other financial organization.

However, a few government programs offer what they allude to as "purchase money loans." In these situations, they employ the second meaning of the term and provide specialized programs that offer credits to buy a house. These loans are gotten through a customary moneylender and sponsored by the government program.

FHA Purchase Money Loans

The least up-front payment prerequisite for purchasing a home with an FHA loan may go for as low as 3.5% in the sales price. A few states offer additional financing to help with the payments up-front and closing costs to enable borrowers to put down zero.

They are guaranteed by the Federal Housing Administration, a division under the American Department of Housing and Urban Development.

Unfortunately for investors, they cannot acquire an FHA loan. All FHA loans are given to borrowers who will possess the home.

VA Purchase Loans

VA (Veterans Affairs) purchase loans are accessible to both non-active and active military persons and their companions in specific situations.

A VA loan is ordinarily zero down payment. However, a borrower can put down any sum. The U.S government guarantees all VA loans. Borrowers are prohibited from paying certain expenses in a VA exchange. Also, this loan can be utilized for home renovations and new constructions.

Definition of Purchase-Money Mortgage

The purchase-money mortgage (otherwise referred to as owner or seller financing) is a home loan granted to a purchaser by a seller of a given property. Mortgages of this type are important to real estate transactions where the purchaser has experienced issues getting authorized for credit with more conventional moneylenders.

How to Use the Purchase-Money Morgages

There are a few kinds of purchase-money mortgages with various terms, so investors should comprehend what they're getting into before diving.

Firstly is a direct land contract in which you make an advance installment and concur with the seller on terms, like the interest rate and the mortgage's length.

Comparative agreements comprise lease-to-own homes. Contingent upon the agreement with a lease-to-own family, you get to decide between (rent-option agreement) or obligation (rent-buy agreement) to purchase the house during the rent or when it terminates. Similarly to a land contract, this is quite helpful if you can't get a home loan.

Both lease-to-own and land contracts have advantages like the capacity to qualify for the loans, even with poor credit records. Also, there's the advantage of agreeing to a price tag before the values go up. Be that as it may, there are unmistakable disadvantages.

While you're acquiring seller financing via any mortgage on purchase money, it's typically because you can't qualify for funding somewhere else. As a result, sellers may request a higher initial installment, closing costs, and higher interest rates.

How it works will rely upon the kind of purchase money mortgage you consent to. You will not get the title instantly if it's a land contract. However, it's released once it's either renegotiated into a customary home loan or the last installment is paid. If it's a rent-purchase agreement, you'll get an equitable title. However, you need to purchase as the rent ends.

The legal document for how they're set up will differ from state to state, so make certain to check the local laws for the correct structures. Also, endeavor to consult a lawyer in case you have any inquiries.

In Purchase-Money Mortgage Agreements, What Happens to Existing Mortgages?

Firstly, in a situation whereby you assume the other individual's loan, one could wind up making two payments with different interest rates. The existing mortgage is yours. However, the sale price is usually higher than the current home loan balance you have to pay.

When this occurs, you'll have a separate agreement with the seller regarding the term and the interest rates.

Secondly, if you've planned to accept the existing home loan formally, you'll be required to qualify with the mortgage organization. This means you'll need a good credit record and also keep your DTI (debt-to-income) in a sensible range.

The issue here is that the vast majority are searching for a purchase-money mortgage since they can't meet all requirements for a normal loan.

The Dangers of Purchase-Money Mortgages

There are a few possible dangers to purchase-money mortgages that every investor ought to take note of, and there are:

- Higher sale price and monthly payments: One of the things you have to note regarding purchase money mortgages is, sellers are challenged higher risks by taking care of the financing. Therefore they may demand higher sale prices, thereby leading to higher payments.

- Increased interest rates: If a dealer can't charge a more exorbitant price for facing the challenge, he or she may charge higher rates on interest than what a standard home loan charges. Sometimes, both cost and interest rates might be higher.

- Increased foreclosure risk: The danger of foreclosure is heightened in a few different ways. In a conventional home loan, the moneylender won't show you out for missing one installment. Contingent upon the details of your purchase-money mortgage, dealers could do this, and you would lose whatever money you've paid.

- Might lose the house even if played your part well: If you decide to pay monthly to the seller while they make their payment on the existing mortgage, you're endangering yourself. How? You're trusting that they'll make those installments to the home loan organization. Now, if they don't, they lose the house, and you still get kicked out.

Ways to Qualify for a Loan with the Customary Lenders

Given the stark disadvantages of a purchase-money mortgage getting credit through a conventional moneylender can be appealing. Nonetheless, if you've been experiencing difficulty qualifying, there are steps you can take to change the narrative.

Since conventional mortgage loaning will offer you better terms, it's more appealing to make attempts to get one instead of going for purchase-money. The following are the things loan specialists consider and how you can improve your odds for endorsement.

Establish a Strong Credit History

Possibly, you can't get a home loan based-off the fact that you're new or moderately new to credit. Maybe you've had a few imperfections previously and are making moves to start afresh from the beginning. Whatever the case, constructing a solid record of loan repayment will better your odds of qualifying.

The question then is, how can you do that? Well, guess what? It's nothing out of the ordinary. Here are a couple of things to do:

- Start little: If you've never had credit, you may need to work with your bank to get either a certified credit card (with your money in it) or a "credit-building" private loan that's paid back in bits. From then onwards, you can stir your way up to customary credit cards just as well as auto loans and a home loan.

- Pay as at when due: A sizable segment of your FICO assessment depends on making on-time installments. Late collections & payments or charge-offs can hurt your record.

- Do not spend beyond your needs: You need some level of debt and credit use to improve to as regards future moneylenders and creditors that you can deal with it mindfully. Be that as it may, your credit use ought never to surpass over 30%, and you need to hold Debt-To-Income (DTI) under wraps.

- Mix It Up: Creditors and banks need you to show a blend of the various kinds of credit. Revolving debts are those where the one with a changing balance monthly (think on credit cards). The installment loans include a preset balance that's paid-off after some time, like the auto loans.

Improve Your Credit Score

If an individual follows the steps listed above you have a decent foundation for improving your credit score. Past that, there are two or three further steps you can take to step up your credit record.

- Pay down/off debts: This correlates to estimations of obligations and credit use. If it's difficult to understand current deficits, you can attempt to work out something with the lenders. Accepting payment isn't the best for your score. However, it's still better than nothing.

- Monitor your credit: It's a smart thought to consistently screen your credit, both for the motivations behind following up on\your growth and fixing any blunders you may find that could be hauling your score down.

Although you'll have more choices if you have a decent credit assessment, there are still customary credit options that won't require much stress. It's possible to get FHA loans with a credit score as low as 580 and a 3.5% upfront installment. If your score is from upwards of 620, you can have a higher DTI, which may add to your budget.

VA credits are accessible to qualifying service members, veterans, and enduring life partners only. You needn't bother with an upfront installment. The VA doesn't have a base credit score prerequisite. However, banks set their approaches.

Improve Your DTI

Debt payments are unfathomably significant as far as your DTI is concerned. DTI is a key measurement for moneylenders doing a wide range of credits because the lower it is, the greater limit you need to get monthly payments.

DTI is a proportion communicated as a percentage which analyzes your current revolving and debt installments to your pretax month to month pay.

The key here is to remember that, to be selected for good home loan alternatives; it's a smart move to keep your DTI at or beneath 43%. Nonetheless, FHA and VA advances permit you to be endorsed with even higher debts.

Develop Your Savings

It's indispensable to special attention to your investment funds when attempting to meet all requirements for a home loan. First off, there's the initial payment. If you do not fit the bill for a VA credit, the most you would possibly be needed to put down is 5% of the price tag on a standard mortgage.

Past that, you'll likewise require reserve savings. The reserves are various home loan payments that you could manage in critical situations of emergencies and the likes. The amount you will need for later use relies upon the sort of credit you're getting.

Seller Financing

This can be a valuable instrument in a tight credit market. It permits merchants to move a home quicker and get a sizable profit for the venture. Also, purchasers may profit from more adjustable rates and better terms on a home loan.

The sellers who are ready to assume the lender's function are not much, everything being equal, let's say maybe under 10%. Be that as it may, sellers can lessen the inherent dangers by playing it safe and getting professional assistance.

The Mechanics of Seller Financing

Seller financing requires the seller to assume the part of the loan specialist. Rather than offering money to the purchaser, the seller stretches out enough credit to the purchaser at the home's buy cost, short any initial installment. The purchaser and dealer sign a "promissory note" containing the details of the credit. Then the purchaser repays the advance after some time, obviously with interest.

These are typically short-term credits. The idea is that within a couple of years, the home will have increased enough in value, or the purchasers' financial status will have improved enough that they can renegotiate with a customary moneylender.

From the dealer's outlook, the brief timeframe period is additionally useful as sellers can't depend on having a similar future as a mortgage loaning foundation. They probably don't have the persistence to wait for about thirty years before the credit is paid off. Moreover, sellers would prefer not to have to deal with the dangers of extending credit longer than should be expected.

A seller is in the best situation to offer this bargain when the house is mortgage-free and clear of any debts.

Kinds of Seller Financing Deals

Here's a glance at probably the most widely recognized kinds of seller financing.

- *All-inclusive mortgage*: In a comprehensive home loan or an all-inclusive trust deed (AITD), the seller conveys the promissory note and home loan for the whole balance of the home cost.
- *Junior Mortgage*: In the present market, banks are hesitant to fund over 80% of a property's value. Sellers can stretch out credit to purchasers to compensate for any shortfall:

    The merchant can convey a second or "junior" contract to balance the house's price value. For this situation, such a seller quickly gets the returns from the principal contract from the purchaser's first home loan. Nonetheless, the seller's risk in conveying another home loan is that the individual gets a lesser priority should the borrower default.

The dealer's second or junior contract is paid simply after the primary moneylender is paid off and satisfied with the deal in a repossession or foreclosure. Likewise, the bank may not consent to make a credit to somebody that has so much unpaid debt.

- *Land contract:* Land contracts do not give a title to the purchaser. However, they do provide the purchaser an "equitable title," a briefly shared possession. The purchaser makes installments to the seller and, after the last installment, the purchaser gets the deed.
- *Rent option*: Here, the seller rents the property to the purchaser for a contracted term (similar to a standard rental); however, that seller additionally consents (as an advance fee) to offer the property to the purchaser by some predetermined time in the future. A few or the entirety of the rental installments can be credited against the price tag. Different realtors use varying tactics on rent options.
- *Assumable mortgage:* This kind of home loan permit the purchaser to assume the dealer's position on the current home loan. Some FHA and VA loan programs, and even customary ARM (adjustable mortgage rate) loans, are, with the bank's endorsement, assumable.

Getting Professional Help

Both the purchaser and dealer will probably require a lawyer or a realtor (or even both) and some other qualified guru in seller financing and home exchanges to review all property agreements. The promissory note and some other fundamental desk work need to be reviewed as well.

What's more, announcing and paying expenses on any seller financed arrangement can be muddled. The dealer may require an expert on taxes to give guidance and help on the deal.

Tips to Minimize Seller Risk

Numerous sellers are hesitant to guarantee a home loan since they dread that the purchaser will default on payments. Be that as it may, the dealer can find a way to lessen the danger of default. A decent expert can assist the seller in carry-out the following:

Require a credit application: The dealer should demand that the purchaser complete a nitty-gritty loan application and altogether check the data the purchaser gives there. That incorporates running a credit check and reviewing business, resources, budgetary cases, references, and other foundational details and documentation.

Enable seller to endorse the buyer's finances: The sales deal (that determines the arrangement's particulars alongside the loan amount & terms, and interest rate) ought to be made based on the dealer's endorsement of the purchaser's financial circumstance.

Secure the loan with the home: The loan ought to be ensured by the property. That way, the lender (the seller) is empowered to foreclose the home if the buyer defaults. The property should also be assessed to affirm that its worth is equivalent to or higher than the price tag.

Get an advance payment: Institutional moneylenders request initial installments to give themselves something to hold against the danger of losing the venture. It likewise provides the purchaser with a stake in the property and makes them less inclined to leave whenever there's any difficulty. Dealers ought to do the same and gather, at any rate, 10% of the price tag. If this is not done, foreclosure could mean the seller is left with a property that cannot be sold to cover expenses in a delicate and falling business sector.

Negotiating the Loan

Same as a traditional home loan, a purchase-money loan is negotiable. To concoct an interest rate, think about current rates that are not explicit to singular banks. Make use of the services on websites like Bankrate and HSH to check daily and weekly rates in the property region. Note you should not fit for available rates. Be ready to offer other investors decent interest rates, low initial payments, and different concessions to draw in purchasers.

Since sellers ordinarily don't charge purchasers with points (each point is 1% of the advance sum), commissions, yield spread premiums, or other home loan costs are usually affordable. They can likewise offer less stringent qualifying measures and advance payment stipends.

That doesn't mean the seller should accept all the whims of the purchaser's. Sellers additionally have the privilege of a good return. A positive home loan that accompanies not many expenses and lowers regularly scheduled installments ought to be converted into an honest evaluation for the home.

Employing a Loan Service Company

To help facilitate paperwork issues, dealers can employ a "loan servicing organization" to help draw up the home loan, mail explanations to the purchasers, gather installments, and generally manage the mortgage.

Chapter 12 – How to Form Partnerships to Invest in Real Estate with Little Money

Investment partnerships are unique systems for bringing in lots of real cash. Purchasing an investment property with a partner has to do with at least two people who have agreed to pool their skill, money, and different assets to invest in properties. Properties range from condominiums, single-family homes, lofts, or multifamily homes.

Partnerships may be arranged in Limited Liability Partnerships (LLPs) or Limited Liability Companies (LLCs). From a more extensive perspective, investment property partnerships can be classified into the following groups.

- *Active partnerships*: With this real estate partnership's structure, every partner is included effectively in the business's everyday running. For instance, one partner could be responsible for financing, while another administers the property board. The key to this type of partnership property is to permit each investor to work in the fields where they're most effective.

- Passive partnerships: Investment property partnerships can be an extraordinary method for raising capital for a real estate venture. In this course of action, one partner has the skill and knowledge, so he/she does the work while another has the capital, thereby supplies the necessary financing. The partners will have to agree as to how they intend to share the profits.

In any real estate partnership venture, commitment is not something to be trifled with, rather as a vital factor in effective real estate business. Having a good partner to deal with could most certainly be the best choice you make. In any case, having a poor real estate partner will disable progress.

Keeping that in mind, it's to your greatest advantage to mind due diligence and take as much time as is needed screening all possible partners. It is at that level that you can truly appreciate the value of a great partnership.

With such an amount of wealth on the line, what's the best approach to deciding the best real estate partner for you? The best way to go about this is moderately basic: get your work done and don't hurry into anything without being sure beyond a shadow of a doubt. In case that is insufficient to get the ball rolling, there are a couple of more things you ought to do (and not do) to ensure your partnership deal is well organized. How about we investigate probably the most significant do's and don'ts when it's time for you to move into real estate partnerships.

What is a RELP?

A RELP (real estate limited partnership) is the more simple arrangement of real estate partnerships. As indicated by Investopedia, a RELP is a body that offers a platform to put resources into a diversified real estate investment portfolio. Real estate partners will decide how the business runs and is finally taxed by the government. While the structure of a RELP may seem a little contrasting, they are practically identical to other real estate partnerships, for example, REITs and the managed total estate-focused investment funds.

Expected returns regularly measure essentially high. Nonetheless, they additionally convey high risks. RELPs are promoted with well-defined particulars of the substance, plans, and the general method for sharing profits. As a rule, RELPs is targeted at institutional investors or people with high asset values.

Most partnerships in limited real estate have an explicitly characterized focus on their business plan, whether it be for developing a private area or business-to-business structures. In many cases, RELPs specialize in explicit real estate fields and projects, for example, retirement houses or high-end commercial businesses.

Is the REIT Classified Among the Limited Partnership?

A REIT (real estate investment trust) isn't among the limited partnerships. However, they are dealt with similarly as the tax agencies deal with the limited partnerships. REITs and limited organizations can both evade twofold tax collection because of their business structures. The two-class blocks vary in manners of execution, including their venture center.

Although REITs are regularly in the financial market, limited companies focus mostly on energy or common assets. One more distinction can be found when you look at the conveyance prerequisites for start either partnerships: REITs compensation sits at 90% of their profit. In contrast, regular associations normally have targets, yet they are not mandatory.

The Commercial Partnerships in Real Estate

Perhaps the ideal way to break into the real estate world is through a fruitful partnership. Commercial real estate raises the stakes higher when contrasted with private ventures. Business properties are bigger and require more financing and more involvement. Nonetheless, the true real estate partnerships deals can permit at least two financial specialists to consolidate their knowledge and money to accomplish the high net revenues these properties can generate.

Real Estate Partnership Taxation

Typically real estate limited partnerships, a.k.a RELP structure goes through a comparative taxation cycle to that of the privately owned real estate venture. Now and again, a RELP could be seen as an organization, which could prompt an alternate tax structure. However, these organizations possess similar features in terms of pay, misfortunes, allowances, and credits. One of the numerous advantages of a partnership agreement is that it gives all persons involved greater adaptability in concluding on how to divide both the profits and losses.

Pros and Cons of Real Estate Partnerships

Real estate partnerships are generally considered great schemes for individuals to fill up the voids and succeed in their real estate endeavors. Those who have either the skills or the finance but are lacking in the other area can seek out allies who can supply the other vital piece to a successful real estate puzzle.

Apart from that, a really strong partnership can go a long way in how new investors can express themselves fully and get off to a strong start. The following are only a couple of the numerous advantages related to real estate partnerships:

- The ideal partner can table additional assets, including capital or a broad network.

- This partnership permits the two players greater adaptability with regards to disseminating benefits and misfortunes.

- Partners can give one another differing and new perspectives while investigating possible deals and arrangements.

- The joined portfolios from all real estate partnerships can help bring the "goodness" factor to the party with imminent moneylenders.

- Partnerships rotate around balance, permitting the two players to isolate and overcome debts and all outstanding tasks.

A decent partnership always that little extra something to the table that an investor might not have right away. Whether it's admittance to capital or market involvement with your favored investment territory, partnerships are not for everybody. Consider the following real estate partnership disadvantages:

- Earnings must be shared between all involved parties, sabotaging profit totals.

- Real estate partner may possess altogether different styles, prompting hierarchical clash.

- If the partners' understanding isn't totally clear, there might be issues appointing duties and losses.

- Partnerships could put a pointless strain on a generally good friendship.

- In a few cases, an involved party may carry more to the table, thereby causing a disparity in value or abilities.

The ideal approach to alleviate these potential clashes is by building up a reasonable arrangement before you begin working together. Remember, a fruitful partnership doesn't occur without any forethought; effective business connections may set aside an effort to create. While they can be profoundly useful for certain, partnerships are not important to maintain a fruitful business. Gauge the advantages and disadvantages before deciding to establish a real estate partnership and pick what is ideal for you.

Ways to Structure Your Real Estate Investment Partnership

How investors structure, real estate partnerships can straightforwardly prompt its prosperity or disappointment. Along these lines, this bit of the cycle ought not to be messed-up by either colleague. You should adhere to the following procedures when you begin:

1. Determine if the potential partnership is appropriate for you
2. Review your qualities and shortcomings
3. Find somebody who praises your aptitudes
4. Evaluate the capability of the organization
5. Create well-defined expectations and roles
6. Establish strong and realistic terms of agreements
7. Keep the cycle straightforward
8. Protect yourself from likely difficulties
9. Review all business objectives together

You have to decide if you need A Partner.

Decide, without question, if you want to get into a partnership. Extremely numerous real estate investors are captivated by the possibilities of cooperating with another person before they even think about the other option. Keeping in mind that one should never forget that as much as partnerships can be incredibly valuable, they can also be fatal. Therefore be cautious, apply thought before deciding to jump into it.

One should understand that you should join forces with another individual only when the other party presents something new that you presently don't have. Maybe the potential partner has a capital or is has an extensive network. Whatever the case may be, recognize what you gain from collaborating and deciding if the advantages exceed the negatives.

Perform some Self Evaluation

Structuring a real estate partnership has more to do with coordinating qualified applicants than everything else. Tragically, numerous real estate investors invest too much energy assessing their possible partners and insufficient time considering themselves. For reasons unknown, both are amazingly fundamental. Indeed, one should maintain an unprejudiced self-assessment similar to when meeting with an applicant.

Self-evaluation will recognize the areas you are weak at present and those where you're strong. Doing this will give you an incredible start when attempting to discover a partner. Once you are positive about what you are good at and can bring to the table, you would define what to search for in an accomplice.

Significantly, you carry out this exercise on yourself and by yourself works as long as you're honest with yourself. Put aside some an ideal opportunity to outline your qualities and shortcomings, and use what you discovered to shape your decision as to needing a partner or not.

Discovering The Right Partner

If no other thing, a partner ought to be entrusted with bringing something new to the table. You are also keeping in mind that it's completely adequate for your planned accomplice to share some of the extraordinary abilities you don't presently have. They should offer a complementary range of abilities. All in all, the accomplice you choose to work with should make up for whatever vital weakness you might have and meet a particular need.

Through the expansion of a complementary range of abilities, your business will become more flexible and more ready to deal with whatever the real estate market throws at you.

Mind Your Due Diligence

Going into real estate isn't anything to trifle with, nor should you do as such without contemplating things from a sound perspective. As stated previously, you should be sure that you are going into a partnership for the right reasons, yet, significantly, you pick the correct accomplice.

In addition to the fact that they should give you credit when something praiseworthy is done to amplify your confidence, he or she should be somebody you trust. In screening your possible accomplice, it's critical that they can take care of their responsibility competently. Additionally, it's dependent upon you to ensure they can. You are the last watchman, so ensure you are agreeable that your accomplice is well equipped.

Set Roles And Expectations

Before going into the partnership proper, it's your greatest advantage to distinguish what will be anticipated from every person and the jobs for each party to do. In doing such, you will alleviate the danger of running into huge issues. It's important that the more plainly you can characterize each accomplice's particular job, the better. In a real sense, there ought to be no disparities concerning what position you will play through the span of the real estate partnership. Who will deal with the funds? Who will be liable for advertising? Which of you will be entrusted with negotiations at the end table?

A partner should realize who is doing what a long time before the circumstance emerges. That way, you can set sensible roles for which each partner will be accountable.

Set Terms

When you conclude how to designate obligations, it's the ideal opportunity for a more chaotic discussion: assigning losses and profits. Real estate partnerships are structured with an agreement that directs the specific terms of understanding for the business. A typical structure will assign what segment of profits are given to the business and how extras will be shared among all involved partners.

For instance, your arrangement's provisions could be to have 40% of the profits kept to maintain the business. Afterward, let's say a 50/50 split between accomplices can follow on what's left on income. There are unlimited ways for the terms of the agreement, be certain both of you find common ground that you two concur on.

Keep It Simple

Keep away from over muddling things as you get into the real business. You have to envision business tasks, yet you don't have to set mid-day breaks yet. Make sure to remain engaged as you arrange and keep things straightforward. In the beginning, it is smart to recollect that one should not go over the edge with complicated plans. All partners need to comprehend what they are getting into expressly. All parties must be present as you all polish your methodology; notwithstanding, you have to see precisely what you are getting into. Work with a land lawyer or any other legal advisors to arrive at a language everybody can get.

Protect Yourself

By now, you should have set up for yourself an ideal business association, yet that doesn't promise it will be sheltered from difficulties. Your partner and yourself should seek protection against unforeseen circumstances. This implies setting up the best possible business structure to secure your resources (whether through an LLC or something different). Protecting yourself likewise tells you and the partner get together to talk about what might occur during any potential business differences.

This incorporates discussing how you both plan to share the spoils and losses. Ask yourselves, what might occur if a partner decides to leave, then come up with a solution among yourselves. Discuss the disintegration cycle of the business. All these terms should then be sealed with a legal advisor and put in the contract. While nobody prays for bad things to happen, the partnership has to consider such possibilities. You and your partner must be secured in case it does happen. It's just as the popular quote goes, "prepare for the worst but still plan for the best."

Set Goals

Try not to disregard your potential partner's long-term objectives. Understanding what your accomplice asks for from this trade is significant, particularly in the case of newbie investors who form partnerships. If nothing else, getting a clear image of your partner's wants from the intended block could make or mar your business relationship is going forward. It would help if you were sure beyond a shadow of a doubt that every one of your objectives is in accordance with everyone's own goals. There is no reason for joining forces up with somebody that has opposing goals. Best case scenario, you will be pursuing different goals hence running in opposite directions rather than going strong in one particular order. At the very least, you could risk destroying the whole partnership.

Chapter 13 – How to Mitigate Financial Loss as Possible

One negative constant in any business is a risk. It cannot be avoided but only managed. Therefore putting resources into real estate isn't a different case. Be that as it may, there are ways to alleviate the risks involved in real estate investment.

Everyone knows (except you're a kid) that it is impossible to forestall all risks related to a business. If there are no outside variables that can trouble the venture, then there are probably natural forces that could trigger losses.

Believe it or not, it is actually what occurs most times in real estate investments. In any case, no one can abstain from losing money, but we definitely can take steps to decrease the dangers involved in real estate investments. Let's discuss the major risks involved in real estate investments.

Real Estate Investment Risks: Bad Returns

Every investor is investing in the business to make profits through real estate. To do this implies that you get a decent quantifiable profit from a property that you've invested in. The most awful thing then is when you invest and end up with bad returns. This implies that you are losing cash as opposed to making it. Therefore, to relieve the dangers of a terrible rate of profitability, you should carry-out what is termed an "investment property analysis." This kind of analysis guarantees that you are purchasing a beneficial property.

Although it doesn't imply that your property won't be influenced by different variables that may decrease profit, you'll at least get an idea of the property's latent capacity.

The most significant numbers that the "investment property analysis" discloses are the rental income just as the rental costs to anticipate. This analysis is an extraordinary pointer to future productivity. You can also utilize this kind of statistical data to calculate your chances of balancing out on a rental property. The lower the rate, the better.

Real Estate Investment Risks: Depreciation

One of the prayers of a real estate investor is that the real estate he buys will appreciate it. When this doesn't happen, then there's trouble. Real estate investors need the value of the property they believe in shooting up as when due, yet, it does happen that a property devalues instead of increasing in value.

To mitigate depreciation, you need to contemplate the area. In different terms, carry-out the real estate market analysis here too. This will examine the appreciation rate in a specific territory dependent on recorded information. It will unquestionably help you discover places where you can confidently purchase real estate with at least an above-average assurance that it will appreciate.

Second, it will help you get an idea of the amount to expect in rental income after you compare your property and other similar rental properties around the area.

Real Estate Investment Risks Vacancies

One of the dangers involved in real estate investments is how to discover tenants. This causes a negative income rather than a positive income considering that a property is a debt, except if it's actively filled. Now, how can an investor go about this? Firstly, ensure you do more than decent marketing. It won't be an issue for the individuals who plan on recruiting a property supervisor. Property managers are land specialists and possess expertise in making a house more engaging to potential occupants.

However, it may be an issue for individuals who are dealing with the property alone. Concocting great advertising procedures would naturally be the best answer. The investor should, however, ensure to learn how marketing works and the best method to practice in your area.

Second, there is the issue of taking care of your bills when you actually can't bring in inhabitants. This could be effortlessly tackled if you have enough money set aside for this purpose before the purchase. Notwithstanding your rental technique, it isn't, in every case, simple to discover inhabitants immediately. Thus, you need to have some money accessible until your property begins to produce some sure income.

Truly, this is one major reason why all newbie investors ought to study the real estate market well before delving into it. In certain areas, rental appreciation is high, which prompts low rental interest. In different spots, the rental part is high because of the absence of rental supply.

Hence, it is best to put resources into places like the second scenario to ensure it won't be a battle to discover inhabitants.

Real Estate Investment Risks: Bad Tenants

Now and then, the dangers of involvement in real estate investments have nothing to do with the expected property profit. Sometimes, it is the awful occupants. This is the bad dream for most landowners out there. Rather than having the income for themselves, they wind up paying for harms these occupants cause.

This inevitably prompts negative income. To lessen the dangers of terrible inhabitants, there are two different ways you could go with:

- You perform tenant screening preceding, giving them access to your house.
- You get a decent insurance policy in place that will cover any potential harms your occupant's cause.

Real Estate Investment Risks: Lack of Knowledge

Indeed, the entirety of the above are risks that an investor has to prepare before investing. Be that as it may, the primary driver of these potential dangers is lack of knowledge. It is general knowledge that you should familiarize yourself with the essentials when you want to begin a venture. You truly need to know where you are going, particularly if it's real estate investments. To mitigate this significant danger, there are numerous websites and ebooks (such as this one) dedicated to teaching all there is to know about real estate.

All the above-stated risk management strategies will limit the odds of losing-out in the business. Still, below are some practices that can help you rake in good profits.

Search for Below-Market Rents when Purchasing

If you can find an investment property with a major part of rents that are less than the prevailing market rates, simply getting the rents up to proper market standard will bring about less risk in your investment because of better incomes.

The capacity to do efficient renovations to improve rents is also a decent marker for acquiring an investment property. Regularly, landowners will get burnt-out on marketing, and they will make do with manageable rents, regardless if they are below current market rates.

This will skew a portion of the valuation and ROI calculations. However, this will be a positive occurrence if you can see it. When there is more lease accessible, actual leases will skew calculations off course.

Search for Advantageous Financing which Reduces Cash Outflow

With assumptions or any other inventive financing solution that decreases, the interest rate is a decent methodology so long as the property isn't over-valued. Bringing down your interest rate by bringing down the financing cost will build income and decrease "real estate leverage risk."

In case you're certain that you will hold the property for, let's say, ten years (more or less), you should check out the ARM (Adjustable Rate Mortgage) for that period. It's a real life-saver when it comes to such matters.

Increase Your Down Payment

With the huge hype around no-down or low-down financing for big gains in real estate investing, it's not hard to make a wrong turn in the real estate world.

At times bringing down your "return on cash investment" is as yet a better solution. High debts may backfire, especially in a time of increased vacancy or credit loss.

Raising your up-front payment will take more money forthright. However, it will decrease the sum financed as well as the lower payments. When prices are reduced, income goes up. Then refinancing is a future option.

Search for Real Estate that You Can Profitably Improve

Expanding a property's value through enhancements builds value and also leads to an endless supply of resources. Should loan costs decline, the expanded worth can likewise fund different ventures or diminish debt service.

The correct improvement choices can likewise pull in better inhabitants and legitimize higher rents. The ROI on capital put into the renovations can be appealing.

Search for Future Hot Areas

Finding an area that is going to be "the hot cake" can be very beneficial. Recognizing a local that is currently developing and rehabilitating places you ahead to gain from property appreciation.

The current surveys reveal that both the younger and older home buyers and the renters prefer to live near the city areas. These are most times more senior communities, and improving old homes can be gainful.

The Basic Ideology is to Purchase Value

The time and energy put into finding a property valued below the market price are typically well justified, regardless of the sacrifices. This is key, and although it's easier said than done, there's no running away from this truth.

Conclusion

A lot of non-investors have developed a bunch of myths about real estate investors and their investments. A major one is the belief that investing is very complicated and requires someone smart and sophisticated.

If you've come this far in this book, you should already know by now that investing can be quite easy and uncomplicated if you learn the ropes well. There are simple dos, don'ts, and general principles to follow, and here in this guide, we've laid it all on the thick for you. So what's next? ACTION!!!

It's time to set the ball rolling. Through the numerous loans that we've listed as available, you know now that money is not a problem. If your credit score seems a problem, we've detailed ways to improve it to access loans. We've also listed many free online tools that would make it all easy, and you can even put some of them on automatic.

Now you know the people you need in your corner, for instance, the contractors, the expert realtors, and so on. We've also given you an idea of places to look for cheap and profitable real estate. With this book, you've learned ways to deal with renters (if you're doing rental properties). Also, you've known how to flip a house and so on.

All in all, this book (Zero to Millionaire Real Estate Investor) and your determination to put it to good use is all you need to start and finish your journey as a millionaire real estate investor.

"If you have enjoyed reading this book, I would be very grateful if you could post an honest review on Amazon. All that you need to do is to click the blue link next to the yellow stars. On the left, You'll see a gray button that says "Write a customer review"—click that and you're good to go, thank you."

Johnath

www.ingramcontent.com/pod-product-compliance
Lightning Source LLC
Chambersburg PA
CBHW060843220526
45466CB00003B/1214